THIRST

Quenching Your Deepest Desire

C. WESLEY KNIGHT

THIRST

Interior Layout Design: OA.Blueprints, LLC

ISBN: 978-0-692-88375-4

CONTENTS

DEDICATION

To the love of my life, Stephanie. Thank You
for believing in me when I doubted myself. You are more
than my wife. You are my inspiration.

To My Awesome children, Aja and Ajani, I love you with
all my heart. I am extremely proud of who you are and
what you are becoming.

To my late grandmother, Mum Knight.
I miss her love and wisdom.

THIRST

ACKNOWLEDGMENTS

Mama Stiney, (my spiritual mother) and Walter Brown, Elder Lester (my spiritual father) and Lee Scott, Uncle Charles (my ministerial father) and Vivian Joseph, T. Marshall Kelly (mentor), Minister Kwame Vanderhorst (mentor) and the late great Mama Bliss (adopted grandmother)

Thank You for Just Being You:
Ray and Yen Andrews
Ny and Darren Ruddock
Everett and Kem Roper
Remi Sinclair
Damian Chandler
Kirk and Alison Nooks
Sheldon and Tracy Kay
Uncle David and Auntie Juliette
Jack and Belinda Barnes
Esther and Roy Jones
Dane and Nadine Timpson
Greg and Nicole Glass

Thanks for your guidance, inspiration and support in writing this book:
Dr. Eric Thomas
DeVon Franklin
Dr. Suzanne Clark
Dr. Myron Edmonds
Keith Goodman
Debleaire Snell
Dr. Dion and Dilyn Henry
Drs. Andrea and Kurt King
Dr. Sean McMillan
Jeremy Anderson
Sandra Randolph
To all the Knight family, I love you!

THIRST

PREFACE

Why Another Book About Love and Sex?

Why would I want to write a book about sex? Don't we have enough books about sex? We see it in most of the advertisements on television. We hear it in most of the music that is played and produced. We see sexuality oozing out of horny teenagers and experimenting college students. We think about sex all the time. We have conversations about sex and opinions about sex. Sex is everywhere and affects everyone. It affects the people who are engaged in it. It affects the people who are not getting any. It concerns the married and the single. The young and the old (thanks to Viagra). Sex is probably the most talked about subject other than money. Everyone thinks about it, and everyone has an opinion about it. So why another book on sex? Well, this book is not really about sexuality. It's actually about spirituality in the context of sexuality.

There are many scientists, psychologists and therapists who have taken on the subject of human sexuality, and we have benefited from their wisdom as they have helped us to understand our humanity through the lens of sexuality. The problem is that most books on sex or sexuality deal with the psychology of sex, the physiology of sex, or even the biology of sex. Rarely, if ever, do we discuss the spirituality of sex. Sexuality and spirituality are hardly ever mentioned in the same context and when it is, it is usually with a negative connotation. The very mention of sex and sexuality makes most people blush, causes the heart rate to increase or at least provokes a smile. It just makes us feel a certain way. It evokes our attention. It peaks our interest. In certain settings, you have to whisper when you say it. In other environments, it is expressed much more openly and celebrated. The topic of sexuality just makes you feel a certain way. Passionate. Excited. Expectant. Curious. Nervous. It makes you think of flesh. Skin. Touch. Warmth. It speaks of the ultimate connection to another person.

Spirituality evokes a rather different response. It often draws a disinterested yawn from many people. It conjures up images of meditation and mystical speech. For many people, spirituality makes them think about people chanting or singing weird songs about God or a Higher Power. In many parts of the United States, this word reminds people of going to church, praying, and Sunday mornings. Spirituality usually makes us feel a certain way. Reflective. Quiet. Grateful. Calm. Spirituality speaks of the ultimate connection to what we believe is God. Here's the thing. *What if the two seemingly separate subjects are really the same subject?*

I think we have overlooked the essential spirituality of sex. When I use the term "spirituality" I am referring to the word in its purest and simplest form. Spirituality has to do with not only the religious, but we are talking about the human spirit here. Our spirit has significant impact on how we view and practice our spirituality. The focus on body and mind, without a healthy understanding of the spirit's role in healthy sexuality, is the state of being unbalanced at its best and incomplete at its worst. We cannot talk about sex unless we talk about the human spirit.

This book is about the connection between sexuality and spirituality and how we endeavor to deal with our spiritual desires by pursuing our sexual desires. The two are so intricately connected that it will amaze you. When we separate them from each other, we create a major shift in the human experience. In other words, sexuality without healthy spirituality is incomplete. Also, spirituality without healthy sexuality is incomplete. They are inherently inseparable. In this book, we will explore these connections from a Christian perspective. In this book, we will look at the vital connection between the two as we look at the totality of humanity (mind, body, and spirit). Sex is not just good to us, but it exists for something far greater than us. It symbolizes a divine reality and purpose. We will see that our greatest desires for love and validation are not ultimately met through sexual expression. Most importantly, we will discover why our attempts to use sex to deal with our deepest human needs have always failed and how Unconditional love redeems our spirituality and sexuality. But before we begin, I want to introduce you to a very special woman.

1

THIRST

"About the sixth hour, a woman came to draw water…"

et me tell you a story about a woman. This woman comes to the well one day to get water. She gingerly makes her approach to the well, dancing in and out of the shadows created by the rooftops she passes under. The sun was at its zenith in the pale blue sky, and everyone sought shelter from its rays at this time of the day. But not this lady. She is driven to the well. Not by her need for water. If she needed water, she would have come earlier. All of the other women come to the well in the morning to get water to aid in the making of breakfast, washing clothes, and bathing children. But this lady comes for more than water. She comes to be alone. The well at noon is the only place she knows she can be alone. And this time when she gets there, to her devastation, a man is sitting by the well. Now her plan for isolation has been thwarted. She does not intend to speak to the unidentified man. She will get her water and go. But the man interrupts the awkward silence and asks her to let down her bucket to fetch him some water. Men don't usually come to the well. That is thought of as a woman's job. She could tell that he was a Jew from his clothing. His clothing identified him as a religious teacher. His presence made her a bit nervous because of the tense relations between her people and His people. He also made her nervous because his presence was disturbing her isolation. So she asks him, "Why are you talking to me?" She wasn't being rude. In fact, she did not realize that her internal question escaped from her mind and on to her lips. Before she knew it, she was wondering out loud how a man like him could be talking to a woman like her. Her question was a question of value.

This man was not supposed to be at the well anyway. But he was there for a reason. The Ancient Jews had such a hate for Samaritans that they created a path around the region of Samaria so they did not have to even risk running into one of them. But this man had to go through Samaria on this particular day. He had to meet this woman. She didn't know it yet, but she needed to meet this man. This is no regular Jewish man. This is Jesus. And this was no chance encounter. He got to the well before this woman showed up because that is what He always does. His presence is always where you need it before you get there.

Jesus tells her that if she only knew whom she was talking to, she would have asked Him for what He had. But He doesn't look like he has anything that can help her get what she needs. He doesn't have a bucket to dip into the well. She looks at Him and wonders what He has to offer. Her need is so great, but He doesn't seem to have what it takes to provide what she came to receive. He promises something called "living water". She believes that He is talking about spring water that flows from a natural spring. Everyone knew that natural spring water was much better and fresher than well water. What she does not know is that what Jesus is offering is much better than she could imagine. She questions his ability to deliver on His promise of spring water. She knows in order to accomplish that, He would have to go deeper than the well goes. Somehow this woman knew that the most satisfying things come from the deepest places. Receiving the most satisfying water would require deep digging. She doubts His ability based on her belief that this well she has come to fetch water from is special. This well has historic significance because their ancestors gave it to her people. The well was what everyone used to get their needs met. If coming to this well was good for them, it must be good for her. She did not think about the possibility of having the same needs met in a more satisfying way. Nobody ever thought about the possibility that their thirst could be satisfied from a much deeper source. Jesus is offering her something greater than what has worked for her in the past. She asks Him what He will use to quench her thirst. When she looks at Him, Jesus does not seem to have any evidence that He can deliver on His proposal. At least she had a bucket. Jesus had nothing. Nothing but a promise. Nothing but His presence.

She carried her bucket there to get some water. Buckets were instruments used to get the water they needed. Her bucket was empty, but her needs were great. When the water ran out, she would have to come back to the well to get her supply filled again. That was her pattern.

Come to the well
Get her needs met
Run out of her supply
And come back to the same well.

The next day…

Come to the well
Get her needs met
Run out of her supply
And come back to the same well.

This happened every day, every week, every year, for years without end. She is tired. She is not just tired of the work it takes to fetch water from this well. She is tired of the same routine. She is weary of the work it takes to meet her own needs. She is tired of joy leaking out of her soul like a bucket with a small hole in it. She is tired of running out of what she so desperately needs. But that is the nature of the kind of water she is seeking. The water always runs out. It never lasts forever. Jesus tells her that the water she craves will only make her thirsty again. Her thirst was unquenchable because of what she had been using to satisfy it. He offers her something different. Something more. Something deeper. He tells her that He can give her a kind of water that will never run out. He tells her about a new type of abundance. Jesus tells her that He could put the natural spring inside of her soul so that she never has to depend on any well outside of her to satisfy her needs. He could supply an internal answer to her external pursuits. She might have thought, "Here we go again. Another person promising the world and never delivering." She had been down that road before. But something was different about this man.

Something inside her knew He was right. And something inside her knew that He was not just concerned about her thirst for water. Jesus could see that this woman was as empty as her bucket. She needed something to deal with her emptiness. She wanted what He had to offer. She was beginning to figure out that He wasn't talking about water or any type of liquid. This woman was beginning to figure out that this man was offering something immaterial. She begins to thirst for what He had to offer. She was thirsty, and she was tired of being that way. So she asked Jesus to give her this "thing" He promises. It is interesting that she asks for it even though she does not know what it really is. Somehow she believes that He can do what He said He could do because sometimes it's not about knowing; sometimes it's just about believing. So she asks for the water. Jesus' response is startling and revealing. In fact his response seems incongruent with what she requests from Him.

He says, "Go and get your husband and come back".

This seems to be a strange request based on what He was offering. What does her husband have to do with her receiving water for her thirst? Is Jesus changing the subject? Does he want to give this "living water to her man as well"? Not really. In fact, Jesus' act of calling for her husband was to reveal something about the woman. She wanted this spiritual blessing from Jesus, but Jesus could not grant it until she dealt with the reality of who she really was.

She replied, "I am not married".

Jesus already knew this and said, "That's right. I know you aren't married. I know you have been married five times. And I also know that the man you're living with is not your husband either".

What is Jesus doing? Why is he embarrassing her like this? What does it matter who she lives with and who she sleeps with? What does her sexual relationship have to do with her thirst? Everything. It had everything to do with her thirst.

Jesus was not simply offering her a spiritual blessing. Jesus began to address her spirituality in the light of her sexuality. He brings up her sexual relationship just as she tries to receive a spiritual blessing. He challenges her to understand that before she can be spiritually satisfied, she has to address her sexuality. Jesus does not say that she has to fix it. He is not offering her a condition upon which God can receive her. This confrontation is about revealing to the woman something so vital to her spirituality, that Jesus could not let the opportunity pass. Jesus was revealing the connection between her spirituality and her sexuality.

Jesus confronts her with the truth of her situation. This

woman probably does not like what she is doing. She is either a single woman with a married man or a single woman having sex with a man she is not married to. In her culture and in her understanding of God's intention for humanity, she knows she is living a life that is less than idyllic. She is ashamed. She doesn't want to be looked at with judgmental eyes. She doesn't want people to say anything to her. She is running from confrontation. So Jesus does what she is trying to avoid yet desperately needs. She needs someone to hold up the mirror. Jesus knows that His first step to her spiritual renewal is confrontation. She had to confront the truth of the life she was living. But more importantly, she had to confront the reality of why she was living out her sexuality in that way. Why did she have so many failed relationships? Why was she living with and sleeping with this man? One thing was evident. She had not found lasting love. She didn't know love. But just because you don't know love, doesn't mean you don't need it. It doesn't mean you won't go looking for it either. So she found a man, not love. She had tried love before, and it didn't work. So this time it's just sex. It's just hooking up. It's just sleeping together. And now, she is just empty. But her redemption begins with His confrontation. Jesus makes her see who she really is. And more importantly, He makes her see what she is really doing to herself. She is just having sex. And so she comes back to the well to get what she needs. Her thirst could not be quenched. She had to learn the lesson that eternal thirsts cannot be quenched with temporary things. What she did not know was that her thirst was about to be quenched forever.

2

WHY SO THIRSTY?

This woman's story is a true story. But this book is not about her story as much as it is about our story. Her story is our story. We are all thirsty for something. We can't always articulate it. We struggle to explain it. We search all over to find it. This thirst is the deep longing of the soul. This unquenchable thirst has brought out the best and worst in all of us. The thirst is for that which is just as essential as water. Nobody can live without water. It is the most essential element of our natural lives. Our bodies are largely comprised of water. Our brain function depends on sufficient amounts of water in our system. Our ability to live and thrive is determined by our access to water. Water is essential for life. But plenty of people have access to clean water and are not happy in their lives. This is because just as essential as water is to life so is love to the human soul. Nobody can live without love. It is the most essential element of our spiritual lives. You may wonder what I mean by spiritual life. I will explain that in detail a bit later, however, your spiritual life is not a religious experience. Neither does your spiritual life refer to your affiliation with a church. Everyone has a spiritual life. In a real sense, everyone is spiritual. Everyone needs to love and be loved. Our souls need love. Our ability to thrive in life is determined by our access to love. Love is essential for our development as humans. For example, we see this in the development of children. In a Huffington Post article, author Maia Szalavitz talks about how children under the age of 5 are literally dying due to a lack of love. Studies have shown that during the most crucial years of development, the lack of personalized and consistent empathy causes the immune system to be compromised and blocks the stimulation of growth hormones in young children. It is clear that from our earliest years of development, we need love to literally grow and mature in a healthy way. We all need love. The essential thirst we all crave is to be loved and to be in love.

The thirst for love brings with it the other essential thirsts. We all thirst for companionship, security, appreciation, and self-esteem. I believe that when we are truly loved, all of these other essential needs are met. When you are truly loved, you have companionship. When you are truly loved, you are secure. When you are truly loved, you are appreciated for who you are. Your self-esteem is lifted to higher levels. All of these essential needs are met by love. However, this is not just any type of love. The love we crave is a special kind of love. There are generally three things we mean when we are describing love.

Every kind of love, except one, is based on conditions
Philia love is friendship love. We cannot experience this unless there is mutual friendship. Philia love by definition requires mutuality. There is no such thing as one-way friendship. You can love someone as a friend, but if they never treat you with respect, consideration, and appreciation, they are not a friend. The condition for being friends is that both people must be friends with each other. The relationship is reciprocal. Loyalty, spending time together, and sharing signify the expression of Philia love. The condition for this kind of love is that the love has to go both ways.

Then comes the next kind of love. Eros love is romantic love. There is some level of attractiveness or appeal. It may be physical or mental; ideally, it involves both. It may be love at first sight or love that grows over time because the beauty of the 'person' won your heart. Eros love burns with passion and excitement. Eros love makes every inch of your body feel fully alive. It can make you miss meals, try new things you never tried before, and even cause you to spend crazy amounts of money. My wife Stephanie and I were taken over by this wonderful eros love. We dated through long distance until we got married. In those days, you had to pay for long distance fees to call across the country, and because we were in love, we would talk for hours and hours until we ran out of things to say. Sometimes we would do that crazy thing when you just stay on the phone while the both of you fall asleep just to hear each other breathe. How romantic! But then we would get the phone bills. My phone bill was $1200 a couple of times, and she got a $800 bill once! Eros love can be expensive! But that's what eros love does to you. It burns with inexplicable passion. Eros love is also conditional. The condition of Eros love is that there is some romantic or erotic attraction. You cannot really experience romantic love without appreciating the beauty of the other person. The attraction must be intrinsic or extrinsic, or hopefully both. You cannot be in eros love with somebody who does not love you back.

The third kind of love is different. It is called Agape. Agape love is not based on any condition. It is not based on reciprocity or beauty. There are no preconditions or prenuptials necessary. You can experience agape love and not be in love with the person who offers it to you. It's the crazy good love that is just beyond you. Agape love is the purest, most unadulterated form of love there is. This type of love is what we all thirst for. Unconditional love makes us feel value and worth. It makes us feel secure and highly esteemed. We don't desire to show it. We desire to receive it. Agape love is what I call the "original form of love". This is one of the reasons we crave it so much. We crave it because from the very beginning of human existence, we have been loved. In fact, we were created by Love. This kind of love could not have had any conditions for humanity to receive it because we did not exist at the time that this Love decided to create humanity. This love I'm talking about is God.

We were made by Love for love
Simply put, God created us for no other reason than for us to experience His love. We are not the object of God's love because we are beautiful. Neither does God love us because we have been good and loyal friends. We are loved without the regular conditions of love. We have not been loyal to God. We aren't beautiful or perfect in our character. Even our very best is not good enough to satisfy the perfection of God's love. Agape love doesn't love for those reasons. It just loves. He just loves. God doesn't have love. If so, His love would be conditional and could be retracted based on our behavior or conduct. But the Bible says that God is love. The word used here is 'agape'. This is not 'touchy feely' love. This is not starry-eyed nostalgic love. This is not passion-driven love. It is essential love. It is love for love's sake. God's essence is love.

We crave this kind of love, and yet it seems so illusive. We have tried everyone and looked everywhere, but it's so hard to find. May I suggest that we have been going to the wrong wells.

We have been going to the wrong sources. For too many of us, the quest to quench our thirst for agape love and all that it brings has been marked by a frenzied pursuit of only one kind of love. In today's culture, the "well" of Eros love has become the primary "well" we visit to get our 'love' needs met. In fact, many people cannot think about "being in love" without thinking immediately about sex. Sex is certainly a part of love. However, when we make love and sex essentially indistinguishable, we have major problems. This is why some people cannot fathom having a romantic relationship without having sex. Sex is equated with love. Romance has been reduced to intercourse. Intimacy has been reduced to sensuality. The problem is that the well of Eros love cannot quench the thirst for agape love. Sexual expression cannot fulfill the need to be loved unconditionally. If we keep going back to that well, looking for what our souls are thirsty for, we will always be disappointed. The thrill of Eros love will satisfy us for a while, but it always runs out.

So what do we do? We plunge deeper into the same well for deeper satisfaction. We move from relationship to relationship. We trade lovers in for upgrades. We conclude that the relationship we are in must be the problem. But the truth is, we are looking for the right thing in the wrong place. The woman's daily trip to the well is symbolic of our daily pursuit of love that ends with our ultimate dissatisfaction. We enter into a relationship. We expect unconditional love. We are disappointed, and we try it all over again. Our intentions are good, but we are going to the wrong wells. Eros love is beautiful, but it is not made to satisfy your soul's deepest desire. Trying harder at love will not grant you success. Loving harder will not satisfy your thirst. The well you drink from determines what kind of water you get. You cannot expect spring water from a well.

While talking to one of my single friends, he shared with me that the dating scene is really hard right now. I asked him what the challenges are. Are there not enough single women out there? Is it a matter of meeting single women? He remarked that he had no problems meeting women. As we talked more, I asked him what was he expecting out of a relationship. When he told me that he was expecting a woman to be adventurous, funny, understanding, supportive of his busy work schedule, and would make him feel good about life, I quickly discovered that the challenge was that his expectations for relationships were unreasonable. If we are coming into every relationship with all of these high expectations, we are coming into the relationship setting ourselves up for disappointment. You are going to the wrong well.

Many people get divorces today because of "irreconcilable differences". When you peel back the layers of the relationship, you will discover that often one of the spouses feel that their expectations for their marriage had not been met. When I counseled couples that were in the process of getting divorced, I would ask them about their unfulfilled expectations. I expected to hear things like, fiscal mismanagement, sexual betrayal, or physical mal-treatment. But when I would dig deeper to understand the core of what caused their dissatisfaction, I discovered that the expectations of the dissatisfied spouse were often far beyondthe scope of any human being to satisfy.

"She doesn't **make me happy** anymore."
"He doesn't **make me feel valued.**"
"She doesn't **understand me.**"
"He doesn't **make me** feel the way he used to."
"She is not the same woman I married."

If you are saying this to yourself about your spouse, maybe you should consider this. No one else is responsible for your happiness. Your spouse is not primarily responsible for your sense of self-worth. Here's some breaking news. Your spouse will never "fully" understand you. This is not because you are an enigma. It is because you are always changing. Your spouse is always changing. Marriage is the beautiful and messy dance of two people who are constantly evolving and changing while trying to stay in sync with each other. Your spouse is not there to make you feel a certain way all the time. Marriage promises acceptance, security, loyalty, happiness, and support. But marriage is between two imperfect people. Marriage satisfies many human needs, but it cannot satisfy the deepest needs of the human heart. People are not ultimately responsible for your joy in life. Our problem is that we often expect too much from other people who were never meant to meet those deep needs by themselves. Once again, we keep going to the wrong well.

We all want to be loved, accepted, understood, and appreciated. In fact, we all need it. From a developmental perspective, we often expect too much from our relationships because of what was not given to us in our early years. In the book, *Why Love Matters*, Sue Gerdhart talks about how "the adult still longs to be properly taken care of, to be understood without words, and to have needs anticipated without saying anything due to a lack of this type of care earlier in their lives". She says that this can lead those same adults to be prone to remain highly dependent upon others, "hoping that the magical other will make them feel alright". While she may speak from the perspective of those who came from homes where they were not loved or cared for properly, I think the vital connection she makes is beyond the psychological or emotional realm. You may think that you are exempt to this kind of behavior because you came from a loving and caring home environment. The important understanding we can take away from her research is that if we do not truly "feel loved", whether from our childhood or in our adulthood, we will have a high dependence on other people to fill that internal void. That's where most if not all of us struggle. If there is a void of unconditional love, we will seek for it somewhere, and we often seek for it in someone.

Here are a couple of questions that you need to ask yourself. Have my relationships consistently provided what I have been looking for?

Why is it that even the best of relationships still leave one's soul thirsty?

Romantic relationships by nature don't have an endless supply to meet all of your needs. So like the woman, we return for more, and our thirst remains. Why doesn't your romantic experience meet your every need?

Here is the answer. It was never meant to meet your every need. I know those of us who live in developed countries don't really depend on wells anymore, but you have to understand how a well works to understand why our relationships don't satisfy us wholly. Wells by nature don't have an endless supply. Your need for love cannot be quenched by the well of romantic love because that type of love has a limit to its effect on our souls. Your need for love cannot be quenched by the well of friendship love because that well doesn't go deep enough. Our deepest needs can only be met by the deepest love.

3

THE BUCKET

We all know deep down inside what we really need. Our challenge is that we usually don't know how to get what we really need. If true love is what we are really after, then we all use methods of attaining it. Every relationship is designed to supply you with something. It may be companionship, friendship, partnership, security, or acceptance. When we come to the well of relationships, we never come empty handed. We all approach relationships with our own bucket. **Our bucket is what we use to get what we need.** The bucket is what we use to receive what we desire. All of us bring buckets to the well. It is our way of making sure we get what we need from the relationship. We usually have more than one bucket, but we all have used something to get what we want. Some people are really helpful in order to receive the appreciation they desire. They use the "Helpfulness Bucket". Some people use their money in order to "wine and dine" the person they are dating. They buy expensive things to impress so that they can get the payoff from feeling needed. They use the "Generosity Bucket". Other people use emotional manipulation to get what they want. They are needy and require to be rescued all the time. They get their needs met by emoting in a way that makes the other person have to look out for and care for them. They use the "Emotion Bucket". There are many buckets we use to get what we want. The most common and pervasive bucket that is used in romantic relationships is sex. We use sex to get what we need.

We all need to be loved, appreciated, celebrated, protected and valued. To our souls, these things are as indispensible as water is to the body. What we seek in our sexual exploits and escapades is a noble thing. The problem is what we use in order to get what our souls need. Our bucket is pre-marital sex. Our bucket is sex outside of marriage. Living without sexual boundaries and limits are the norm for us. We have convinced ourselves that this is just the way we get what we really want. We have also convinced ourselves that we deserve to get what we want. So we approach the Relationship Well with our bucket. Some men prove their masculinity with sex. That's their goal for using their 'sex bucket'. Some women seek value, security, or power. They get their needs met by sex. We have convinced ourselves that sex can get us everything we really need. This is not always a conscious act. Most people don't go into a relationship saying to themselves, "I'm gonna sleep with him to feel secure" or "I want to have sex to feel more appreciated and valued". The truth is most of us don't even approach relationships with a clear sense of what we need and how we will get those needs met. Our buckets really exist in our subconscious. We end up using sex without even knowing why.

This is one of the reasons why sexual promiscuity and exploration is so prevalent in our culture. You cannot see more than 3 commercials without being exposed to some sexual innuendo. You cannot turn on the radio without hearing a song about sex. You can't go throughout the day without being bombarded by sexual images or thoughts. It is our favorite bucket of them all. If we are honest with ourselves, the reason we are so obsessed with sex is because we have convinced ourselves that sex, rather than love, is all we need to get what we need. The woman from Sychar had been longing for something much deeper in her soul. The empty bucket was symbolic of the emptiness of her soul. She had to keep coming back to the well because whatever she put into the bucket was always running out. This is what she was doing in her relationships. She used her sexual interactions to fill the bucket of her heart. She longed for love, acceptance, approval and kindness. Sex was her bucket. She filled it up, but what it provided for her would always run out. This is why people are so unsatisfied in their relationships when it's just about sex. Sex serves a powerful function, but sex cannot provide everything we need. Here's the thing. Sex does give us access to those virtues and feelings that we desperately desire. Sex is supposed to make us feel secure. Sex makes us feel good. It makes us feel good about ourselves. Sex is supposed to communicate loyalty. Sexallows us to carry away the water of companionship and understanding. The problem is that just like a bucket, there is only so much capacity to sex. If wells don't provide endless supply, then buckets provide even less. Sexual intercourse is meant to reveal and express a deep and abiding love that communicates value and worth. It is a manifestation of a deeper reality. Sex is supposed to make you feel all of those wonderful emotions and comforts, but it is not made to last. The water always runs out. The feeling always wears off. This is why we have to keep getting more, having more, and searching for more. Our obsession is not really with sex as much as it is about what sex provides for us.

Amy Schuumer, the comedienne and TV show star, wrote a book called *The Girl with the Tattoo On Her Lower Back,* in which she describes her experiences of sex and relationships. Amy Schumer shares her one and only "one-night stand" experience She said that she is really not into having one-night stands, but she explained why she chose to have sex with this perfect stranger. Amy talked about how her own insecurity drove her to break one of her dating rules about sex. She said, "Finding out someone I'd dated was gay at that moment in my life was giving me a hard time. I was having trouble feeling like a sexual being and was wondering about my own worth". Amy admits that this is why she slept with someone she barely knew. She was using sex to make her feel better about who she was as a woman. She used it to convince herself that she was still desirable. She used sex to meet an internal and spiritual need. Amy went on to talk about how the use of sex for this purpose is common. She writes, "We've all tried some form of remedy by way of sex and wound up feeling more alone…". Amy Schumer admits that using sex usually makes you feel really empty (even though she thought that her one-night stand experience helped her to feel better in that instance). She used sex as her bucket that night to feel better about herself. We all have our buckets.

The point is that sex is really never "just about sex". We have sex to prove things to people. We have sex to feel better about ourselves. We have sex to stroke our egos. We have sex to seal a commitment. We use sex because it is our way of getting what we want, and it's the only way we know how to get it. This woman obviously had a problem. She had five failed marriages. One failed marriage could possibly be understood, but five divorces were an indication that something went terribly wrong. While in today's culture we would not even blink at the mention of someone being married and divorced five times, it was a huge deal in Jesus' day. In their culture, divorce was not popular at all. The important thing to note here is that the women of those days did not have the right to divorce. So this woman had not filed for divorce, but she had been served divorce papers five times! What does that do to a person? What does that say about a person's worth? No wonder this woman gave up on marriage! No wonder this woman gave up on sexuality inside of marital love. Maybe she didn't even know what it was to be loved.

QUENCHING YOUR DEEPEST DESIRE

So she uses her bucket.
She settles for sex.
It runs out.
She returns to the well.

She kept marrying and marrying so she could finally get her bucket filled up for good. But the love always ran out. The feeling of security and being nurtured always ran out. She gave up on marriage and just settled for the benefits reserved for marriage. Sometimes we keep going back to what we know because it is just what we do. We go back to our Wells. The famous British actor who most recently starred in the first season of *Game of Thrones*, Sean Bean, has been married and divorced four times. In 2011, the Daily Mail Reporter reported that Sean told a Croatian magazine that he had given up on Marriage. He said, 'Of course I believe in love, despite four marriages. There is nobody who doesn't believe in love. But marriage that fits some people but obviously not me.' Sean Bean gave up on marriage because he kept going back to that Well of Marriage and just couldn't find what he needed. Like the Woman of Sychar, he just kept trying the same thing without receiving new results. How many of us do the same thing? We use our sexual relationships to get what we want, but we end up unsatisfied. We just try another relationship. There is something Sean Bean said that is worth our attention. He said, "There is nobody who doesn't believe in love". This is true. Regardless of what you say and how much you may say that you are not going to fall in love again, we all believe in love. Even if you were to say, "I'm not in love. I'm just having sex", you are in essence looking for love. This is why you keep going back for more. You keep searching for something when you haven't found it yet. Sean was right. We all believe in love. Not only do we believe in it, but we thirst for it. It was his thirst for love that made Sean keep going back to marriage for more. It was her thirst for love that made that

Woman from Sychar keep going back to marriage 5 times, and it is our thirst for love that drives us to keep trying to find love in someone else's bed. We all believe in love, and that's why we are thirsty for it. By the way, Sean Bean proposed to his girlfriend Ashley Moore in 2014. Though he sweared he would not try marriage again, he seems to be going back to the same Wells that didn't work for him before.

Isn't it interesting how we keep going back to something that hasn't worked for us expecting something new the next time? Max Lucado tells an interesting story that helps to illustrate this concept. Max recalls while he was in his office one day engaged in his writing, he saw a beautiful bird perched on a tree outside his window. Max was surprised when the bird took off from his perch and flew at full speed towards the window, slamming into the glass. Max watched as the bird slid down the windowpane, shook himself off and went back to his perch on the tree. The bird then repeated the same action. He took off at full speed towards the window, hit the glass, and slid down the windowpane again. Max thought for sure the bird would have learned his lesson by then. But the bird was not easily deterred. That stubborn bird when back to the same perch on that tree and repeated the same action. Max wondered why the bird would repeat this same painful action over and over again until it dawned on Max why the bird would do this to himself. The bird was seeing a reflection of itself in the windowpane. The bird saw an opportunity to be with another bird and went after what he thought was another bird. He pursued what he wanted and got hurt in the process. However, the bird resolved in his bird brain, that he would try again. So the bird went back to the same perch and repeated the painful action again and again. We are much smarter than birds, but we do the same thing in our sexual relationships. We see something we think will satisfy us and so we go after it with all our passion and desire. We get disappointed and hurt in the process, never learn our lesson, and stubbornly try the same actions over again.

The Woman from Sychar had given up on marriage too. Just living with the man would be enough for her. Just living under the same roof would be enough. No commitment. No strings attached. Just sex would be enough for her. But it always ran out. This is the nature of sex when it is divorced from its original intent. Its pleasurable and noble qualities always run out. Jesus knew this. He knew what she was doing. He knew what she was wanting.

Jesus wanted to help her understand that the sexual life she was living was not in tune with the spiritual life she was wanting.

We become our own obstacles to what we really want. Sexual expression alone cannot satisfy the soul's thirst. This woman had a lover, but she was alone. She made love but was not completely loved. Her love life was not meeting her love needs. Maybe you have tried many sexual relationships, and you remain unfulfilled. You used your sex bucket, and the water ran out. Maybe you thought it was you. Perhaps you thought something was wrong with you. The problem is not with you as much as it is that you are expecting your thirst to be quenched by something that cannot satisfy it.

You slept with him, and you are still thirsty.
She gave you her everything, and you are still thirsty.
You followed through with your sexual fantasy, and you are still thirsty.
You binged on those porn sites for hours, and you are still thirsty.
You took her up on her offer, and you are still thirsty.

If you are honest with yourself, you still feel alone. You still feel like there is more. You still feel like something is missing. That's because your thirst is not only to have great sex. Your thirst is not just to have a great time. Your thirst is to be valued, appreciated, affirmed, and validated. Your thirst is to be fully, completely, and unconditionally loved. That is a spiritual thirst.

You cannot satisfy a spiritual thirst with a physical experience.

Don't you think you deserve more? Do you believe there is an experience that can satisfy your thirst? Aren't you thirsty for more?

When this woman came to the Well with her bucket, she was really seeking to be filled in another way. Jesus saw her bucket and knew that she had come there for water. But the good news is that Jesus looked past her bucket. He knew what her bucket was for, but He sensed a greater need in her and was not distracted by the bucket. I'm glad Jesus still looks past our buckets. He knows why we are in those sexual relationships.

He looks past our bucket.
He knows why we sleep around.
He looks past our bucket.
He knows why we are promiscuous.
He looks past our bucket.

Jesus is never distracted by what you do to meet your needs. He simply presents a lasting alternative to your endless pursuit of a thirst-quenching experience. His love for you is greater than what you have done or what you are presently doing. Your bucket does not disqualify you from receiving what Jesus offers. So bring your bucket. When he is done with you, you won't need it anyway.

4

LET'S GET IT ON

(SPIRITUAL ORIGINS OF SEX)

In order to understand this spiritual thirst, we have to understand the origin of this thirst and its connection to human sexuality. The Creator gave the thirst for love to us in the beginning. God gave us this love because He is love. If you believe that God created humanity, then you must understand that we were created from love. Simply put, we were created by Love for Love. The need for love is in our very soul's DNA because we were created by pure and perfect Love. It's hard-wired into the very psyche of every human being. When we understand this as our origin, then we begin to understand why we thirst for love and to be in love. All of us have not only the capacity to love, but also the ability to share our love. **So we are created by Love for love to love.** The thirst for love is essential to being fully human. And the thirst to love is essential to our likeness to our Creator. We should never be ashamed of our need for love. It is why we were created.

After creating the first human being (Adam), God observed that Adam did not have an equal creation to be the object of his affection. God knew that if humanity was created for love, he had to be able to express his love and affection completely. So the first woman (Eve) was created out of Adam to be the object of his affection. God created Adam. God created Eve to be loved by Adam and for Eve to love him. These two original human beings were created by Love to love each other. The epitome of companionship would be realized as God brought the two human beings together. The thirst for love, belonging, companionship, acceptance, and happiness would be communicated through sexual intercourse with each other. Adam and Eve could be no closer to each other than in the moment of intercourse. They could not feel alone while they made love. They would feel security. Sexuality was the creation given to them to help perpetuate what they ultimately received from God's presence. Sex was created so that we would be reminded that we are not alone. Sex was to remind us that we can be ultimately united with another soul. Sex was to be a representation of unconditional love. It was created to allow us to enter into an experience that would remind us how much we are loved. God's intent was that the gifts he gave us were to perpetuate those Godly virtues in our lives. He would satisfy our thirst, but sex would express, perpetuate, and demonstrate our love for the spouse God gave us.

God gave the first human couple the command to "be fruitful and multiply". This was not some command to simply procreate. This was God nudging Adam in the ribs and telling him, "It's time to get it on!" God was the one who initiated the first human sexual act. God did not only condone sexuality and sexual expression, but it was practiced under His approval and in the context of relationship with Him. Sexuality was originally created to be expressed in the context of God's presence. Humanity was given the gift of sexuality as one of our great privileges and responsibilities. We cannot forget that the first act of human sexual intercourse was actually an act of obedience! This means that sexuality is linked to obedience. But it is not to simply be viewed in the sense of rules and regulations. Adam was not only doing it because he wanted to or because he was told to do it. Adam trusted God. When

God told him to "have sex", Adam obeyed out of trust that even though he had never done this act before, God knew what was best for him. Do you see the connection between sexuality and our spiritual connection to God? It was Adam's connection to God that led him to have sex in the first place. His trust in God influenced him to express himself sexually. He had to trust God in order to express himself sexually.

This is crucial to our understanding of how sexuality was originally created and how it has become corrupted. If the first sexual act was promoted, arranged, and commanded by God, then it means that sexuality was to be expressed in an obedient and loving spiritual connection to God. The corruption of human sexuality began when we became disconnected from a loving and trusting God. Sensuality and sex were not corrupted because of porn, sexual abuse, rape, or deviant sexual practices. The problem with sex today has very little to do with what we do. The corruption of sex today has everything to do with who is absent from our sexuality. Sensuality and sex were corrupted in the Garden where God first created it. When you remove God from sex, you have corrupted His gift. The removal of God from sexuality is not the absence of saying his name. (Many people call on God during sex. In fact, that is the only time some people call His name!) The absence of God is the lack of a vital spiritual connection to God that is based on a loving and trusting relationship with Him. When Adam trusted God, he had "God inspired" sex. In fact, we know this because they both were naked all the time, and because of their vital connection to God and each other, they did not even know they were naked. That had to be some great sex. How could they be having sex and not even know they were naked? This seems rather strange because after they had sex, they must have known they were naked. But it is not until they disobeyed God's command to abstain from the forbidden fruit, that they realized they were naked. Their nudity which was previously normal and natural to them, is now a sense of shame. It was at this moment that sexuality became corrupt. Nudity was now shameful. Sexuality had begun to become corrupt.

Let's be clear. Sexuality began its process of corruption when they stepped out of their loving relationship with God. The defining change came not when they discovered their nudity, but when they stopped trusting God. When they took the fruit, they decided that God had been hiding something from them that was essential to their happiness. They decided that instead of living with and for God, they would become as knowledgeable and informed as God so they could make decisions for themselves. When they chose to live as gods rather than live for God, every gift, including sexuality was immediately corrupted. **Simply put, the corruption of sexuality came when we stopped trusting God.** Every problem we have with sexual deviancy, immorality, impurity, abuse, exploitation, and slavery comes from this one reality. When humanity stopped loving God in a trusting relationship, sex went the wrong way. It became self-centered and self-destructive. For too many, sex has become a way of boosting ego, fulfilling a burning desire or even gaining control over someone. Sex has become a tool, a device, and even a weapon. Sexuality is in trouble because we decided it would be enjoyed and used on our terms. When we decide we know what is best for ourselves, we participate in the original deception and corruption of all good things. When humanity stopped trusting God, we took God out of sexuality.

Spirituality vs. Sexuality
It is tragically ironic that the One who creates our sexuality is no longer welcome to be a part of it. God is not welcome in our conversations about sex in today's society. God is

not welcome in our sexual interactions and decisions. God has been regulated to the realm of the religious. We have separated divinity from sexuality.

The challenge is that even though we took divinity out of sexuality, we cannot take spirituality out of sexuality. Sex and spirituality are inseparable. There is a difference between divinity and spirituality. Divinity refers to the presence of God. Divinity is God himself. Spirituality refers to the spirit of God that all of us have in us. Spirituality is related to the thirst for God. Spirituality is part of sexuality because the origin of sexuality is spiritual. Sexuality is primarily spiritual because God created sex. He created it to be a blessing to the human spirit. He created sex as a way of communicating the virtues of God between a man and a woman.

Sex is able to communicate love, trust, loyalty, security, affirmation, dignity, and even worthiness. Sex helps us get these spiritual needs met. The challenge is that the needs are met temporarily. Sex was never meant to be the substance of these virtues but only to communicate them. Sex is not love, but it has the ability to communicate love. Sex is not loyalty, but it can communicate loyalty. Sex is not security, but it communicates security. Our thirst is for these spiritual virtues that are communicated by the act of sex. This is why the Woman at the Well was in that scandalous relationship. She was just trying get her needs met. She didn't realize that her sexuality had huge implications for her spirituality.

Creation of the Image of God
The idea of being created by a benevolent God contin-ues to be debated by philosophers, scientists, atheists and theists alike. Despite your particular understanding or level of acceptance to this truth, there is one truth that we all can agree with. The gift of creation is real because

human beings possess it. Humans are creators. The Bible says that we are "created in the image of God." This is not only a statement about human origins but also about the gift of reproduction that God gave to humanity. The image of God refers to the character, responsibilities and authority that God gave to humanity.

One of the greatest "godlike" gifts that humanity was given was the ability to reproduce ourselves. God commanded the first man and woman to "be fruitful and multiply". God gave this gift to humanity. He wanted them to reproduce themselves. Reproduction was not only meant to reproduce a likeness to the parents, but to reproduce something far greater. Sexual intercourse was originally rooted in the desire of God to reproduce a reminder of Himself exponentially in the earth. The process of sex is literally the reproduction of the image of God in the earth. When we understand this powerful reality, then we begin to understand that the stakes are extremely high when we are talking about the original plan for human sexuality. The gifts of dominion, authority, and "God-image reproduction" were to be the original heirlooms of humanity. With these, God would perpetuate his presence in the earth, as humanity would live to be the object of his affection.

We have the power to help create another image of God. A male and female can have sex, and they have the potential to cooperate in the creation of another human with the image of God. That is powerful. There was one problem. There was another presence in Paradise. The presence of evil was there. Satan tempted the original human beings to break the connection with their Creator. This caused a chain reaction in the earth. The one condition that the privileges were based on had been broken. They no longer trusted God. The effects were immediate. The ground, which used to yield them crops without planting, now needed their human effort to produce crops. The animals that were not threats to humanity began to become dangerous. Some of the plants and herbs that were once helpful to man's health now became poisonous and easy to misuse **The gift of sexuality was also affected by the loss of trust in God.** If sex was the process that God gave to us to perpetuate his image in the earth, there is no wonder that the Enemy of humanity attacked human sexuality. If sex was what God gave us to communicate all the virtues our souls thirst for, then it makes sense why sex is so important to God. He wants to quench our soul's thirst. This is why Jesus was at the well that day. Divinity wanted to reconnect to sexuality. God wants to come back into our sexual relationships. He wants us to trust Him enough to show us what love and sex are all about. Afterall, He is the one who gave us sex. Will you let Him back into your sex life? He wants you to trust Him with your thirst. Are you willing to let God give you the sex life He always dreamed of for you?

5

WHY SEX BELONGS TO MARRIAGE

Jesus never asked irrelevant questions. When Jesus asked the woman about her marriage relationship he was implying her sexuality in her relationship. This is why he mentioned that the man "she was with" was not her husband. Jesus appropriately implies sexuality without crossing the line. In ancient Jewish culture, sexuality was discussed exclusively in the context of marriage. In fact, sexuality was synonymous with marriage. When Jesus brought up her husband, he was really saying, "Let's talk about the one you are having sex with". When the woman said she was not married, Jesus told her that the man she was with was not her husband, even though they were living like they were married. Jesus was calling out her sexuality, in order to talk about her spirituality. She wanted to talk about spirituality in order to get around talking about her sexuality. She didn't understand that Jesus had come to redeem both of them. He came to redeem her sexuality and spirituality.

Jesus confronted the woman about her relationships because our sexuality has important connections to our spirit. The woman from Sychar had been married unsuccessfully so many times that she had stopped counting.But Jesus had been counting. He knew how many times her heart had been broken. He knew how many times her life had been torn apart. His question reveals the fact that she had given up on marriage. More importantly, she has given up on love. So she settled for sex.

Many people have given up on love and just settled for sex. The challenge is that all of the gifts that God gave to humanity were given in a certain context. Authority, power, marriage, and sexuality were all given in an original context of love. When taken out of that context, they become something they were not meant to be. Authority without love turns into dictatorships and oppression. Marriage without love becomes a contract, a silly arrangement of temporary commitment that might as well be called a "really, long sleepover". And sexuality without love is just, well, sex. It's just a pleasurable process that opens up our souls to so many other realities that we are not fully ready to deal with. Inherent in all of these godly gifts are powers that are subtly powerful and potentially dangerous because they are beyond our human ability to control. More importantly, they were made to exist in their original context. Power must be managed by the restraint of love. If love is not the managing force to keep great power in check, the saying comes true, "Absolute power absolutely corrupts." Marriage is a wonderful human privilege, but without love, marriage can be one of the most destructive experiences to the human soul because one is committed to a union that tears you apart rather than brings you together. Marriage is not inherently good for you. Only a good marriage is inherently good for you.

In a Washington Post article written by Elahe Izadi, the case is made for the quality of marriage and its effect on our overall health. In a study funded by the National Institute of Health, Dr. Lui of Michigan State University states, "Married people seem healthier because marriage may promote health. But it's not that every marriage is better than none. The quality of marriage is really important". Sometimes it's better not to get married than to be in a bad marriage. When love is lost in a marriage, the gift of marriage can become a curse. The same principle applies to sex. Sexuality taken out of its context, while it may be pleasurable and aesthetically beautiful, can be dangerous and hurtful.

It is interesting to note that sex was originally practiced in the context of a relationship. This may not seem significant at first because some would say that most people having sex are in a relationship, even if it's just a "sexual relationship". However, the relationship that sex was first experienced in was no ordinary relationship. It was not just two willing and able adults. The relationship was not simply based on consent or ability. The relationship was a marital relationship. This speaks to the fact that marriage was the original context for expressing one's sexuality. But the relationship did not stop there. This original marriage relationship involved the presence of God. Adam and Eve were not trying to make the relationship work by themselves. God was an integral part of their union and commitment to one another. Marriage was never intended to simply be between two people. It was originally intended to have 3 people involved. Man, woman, and God. **Marriage is the original threesome.**

When we speak of the original context of sex as love, we are not referring to the love that we often speak of in our culture. Lots of people legitimately claim they are in love. Many non-religious people practice monogamy. They will tell you that they are in a "loving relationship". I don't doubt or minimize the truth of that statement. To a certain extent, I can respect that commitment since I know a lot of Christians who are married and are in neither monogamous nor loving relationships.

However, the love that we are speaking about is not a regular love. The love that sets the context for sexuality was the kind of love God has for all humanity. This kind of love is an unconditional love that transcends the parameters of romantic love. God is described as love. This very important distinction is insightful. If God is love, then what kind of love is He? He is the ultimate love that encapsulates and perfects all other types of love. He is love without boundaries and conditions. He is love in its purest form. He is what is called "Agape" love. This is where sexuality was birthed. God, who is the purest form of love, gave us sexuality to be an expression of His type of love. Sexuality was meant to confirm and perpetuate the movement from the lower forms of love to the greatest level of love. When we remove Agape love from the picture, the power of sexuality is minimized and corrupted from its original intent. Sexuality without Agape love is the corruption of the beauty of sex. It becomes something quite different.

Here is the thing about Agape love. The only human construct that best requires showing Agape love to another human being is marriage. Marriage is the school in which a man and a woman learn how to love another person the way God loves them. This is by design. Marriage requires a lifetime commitment to another person regardless of what may happen in the future. The marriage vows that we use at most weddings are a vow to Agape love because they include promises to love without conditions and with-out exceptions. If sexuality is a product of Agape love, then we understand that the only place for sexuality to be expressed in its fullness and beauty is marriage.

Now someone may think that we are supposed to share Agape love with everyone. And if so, this idea of sexuality as an expression of Agape love may lend to the idea of "free love" or "open sex". So let's be clear. Agape love is not synonymous with sexuality or sexual expression. Agape love or God's love can be expressed in selfless service to those who cannot repay us or return the favor. We are called to love everyone like Jesus showed the love of God to everyone. But the marriage institution is different because it simulates the most challenging and potentially rewarding model of bringing two individuals into Agape love. When you are serving and helping people, you can show them love by serving them. If they make you angry or upset, you can serve them and then leave them behind as you return to your personal life. When you are married, you cannot leave your spouse behind. The requirements of forgiveness, selflessness, and showing mercy are required in marriage at a level that no other relationship requires. So in a real sense, marriage provides the most challenging and rewarding opportunities to learn how to love like God does. We are supposed to have sex in that environment of commitment to Agape love.

We also must consider that sexuality also points to the ability of two separate people becoming one. This oneness can only be fully expressed and realized in agape love. If you are going to become one with a person, you have to understand that they will remain different and unique even while they are becoming one with you. This reality of their uniqueness and your collective oneness will require God's love to understand them and live with them. When God gave the first human beings the gift of sex by saying, "Be fruitful and multiply", He did so with the intent that His love would be the foundation upon which that love relationship would flourish. If we cannot learn to love our spouse without God, and sex was created as an expression of that love to our spouse, then we cannot have "good" sex without God.

You want to have sex with your "growth partner". Agape

love requires each person to grow. You cannot make love to someone who is not committed to growing with you. The only person who can make that commitment to grow with you is the person who is committed to a lifetime with you. Thus, marriage is the place where two people grow into love. Marriage is the state of commitment to each other and to the process of becoming a selfless, unconditional lover. **Marriage is the only safe place to express yourself sexually.** When you are making love to your growth partner and not just a sex partner, you are making love to a person who is committed to becoming less selfish. Without the commitment and power of marriage, sex is divorced from its original context and thus loses its power to communicate trust and faithfulness.

THIRST

6

THREE INGREDIENTS TO SEX

(BODY, MIND, AND SPIRIT)

Sex is not simply physical because we are not only physical beings. We are spiritual. We are mental. We are physical. The issues we have with sex today are because we only see the sexual act from one dimension of the human experience. When God created us, we were made from the dust of the ground. Our bodies were formed from the dirt. This is why at funerals you will hear the priest or preacher say, "earth to earth, ashes to ashes and dust to dust". The physical body is what we use to engage in sex. Our obsession with the physical body is evident in all of our art forms. We idolize the curves and bulges of the human anatomy in our music, paintings, sculpture, and media outlets. But sex is much more than the physical.

Sex is much more than physical intercourse. Sex is mental because part of being human is to have superior mental capacity. We have minds that direct, orchestrate, and manage our physical experience. Our mental decisions lead to our actions. Sexual intercourse includes thoughts, fantasies, and urges. The mind is the headquarters of our emotions where we process our desires, thoughts, and impulses. We have to be in the right frame of mind to have a good sexual experience. If you are too stressed out, it affects your body functions. If you are depressed, it will affect your energy level. Your mental and psychological state has direct impact on the physical state. These truths are commonly understood. Whenever we talk about sex, we talk about the physical nature of sex or the psychological affects of sex. But our humanity is not limited to the physical and the mental. There is one more component to the human experience that we rarely, if ever talk about when we talk about sexuality. Every human being is also spiritual.

When we talk about spirituality, we may think about religion or the supernatural. Spirituality has many labels. The spirituality component I am talking about is the spirituality that humanity was given from the very beginning of time. God created us with a human spirit. In fact, the Bible says that it is this spirit that gives us life. God breathed into Adam the "breath of life", and he became a living soul. This "breath" is the spirit that every human being carries in them. We are body, mind and spirit. There are several texts that talk about the connection and synergy of these three components.

Job said, "There is a spirit in man."-Job 32:8
Hannah had a sorrowful spirit- 1 Samuel 1:15
Elisha asked the prophet Elijah for a double portion of his spirit- 2 Kings 2:9
Our spirit can be dedicated to God.—Psalms 31:5
Your spirit can hold malice. -Psalms 32:2
Your spirit can be right or wrong. -Psalms 51:10
Your spirit can be broken. -Proverbs 17:22
Your spirit can be overwhelmed. -Psalms 143:4
Your spirit can be willing. —Matthew 26:41

We all have a spirit.

The spirit of man is where we understand spiritual things. Our spirit is where we connect to divinity. We can discern and appreciate the deepest things of God in our spirit. While the spirit of humanity cannot be understood by science, dissected by methodology, or understood by philosophy, it is as real as the mind or body. The most important thing to know about the human spirit is that we experience life primarily in our spirit. Have you ever felt sad when nothing was right in your life? Have you ever felt something that you could not understand? Have you ever felt a deep emotion that wasn't connected to any event or circumstance? You just felt uncomfortable. You just didn't feel peaceful. Or have you ever felt a great sense of gratitude and contentment about your circumstances even though they were not perfect? That is your spirit. Some people have called this intuition. Others have named it instinct. The Bible calls it your spirit. The spirit is how you sense the intangible. The spirit is how you initially connect to God. The human spirit is where your thirst for love primarily lives. Our thirst for eternity and the eternal comes from our spirit. Our thirst for love, acceptance, security, belonging, and truth resides in our human spirit.

Your spirit is where you long for the things that only Love can give you. This makes sense that your spirit would be the place where you long for God. God gave us this spirit. The human spirit comes from God. The very nature of our spirit is that it longs for the one who created it and gave it to humanity. There is a very powerful truth we must understand as it relates to understanding the role of our spirit in our lives. Everything we truly need to be fully whole and complete is a spiritual need. Simply put, our deepest needs are the needs of the human spirit. One of my first spiritual mentors, Minister Kwame Vanderhorst, helped me to understand a very powerful principle that I believe will unlock a whole new reality for your life. Vanderhorst wrote "that all human life has been designed from center to circumference." The spirit is the deep center of human existence. The mind is the next level moving out from the center. The body acts like the outer realm of human life. In other words, we live from spirit to mind to our bodies. This is significant to our understanding of human sexuality.

Our spirit inspires the mind.
The mind processes what the spirit offers.
The body acts it out.

The spiritual inspires the mental, and the physical is simply a result of what the mind tells it to do. This means that all of our lives are designed to primarily be spiritual. This is a revolutionary way of understanding life. Life is spiritual. Then it is mental. And finally it becomes physical. Do you see how this relates to our sexual pursuit of love? We have used physical sexual intercourse as a means to meet our spiritual needs. We use the physical in order to meet the needs of our spirit. If the virtues we seek flow from the spirit to the mind and finally the body, then why do we focus so much on the physical? We have reversed the process. We are trying to meet our needs by starting from the circumference in hopes that it will reach our center. This explains why sexual intercourse doesn't satisfy the souls deepest need. Sex outside of God's original intent only goes so deep. It may satisfy the physical needs. It is pleasurable and stimulating. It may even meet your mental needs. Good sex can relieve stress and communicate positive thoughts. But pre-marital and extra-marital sexual intercourse cannot meet your spiritual need because they are practiced outside of the context of love that feeds your spirit. You cannot live life from the circumference to the center.

Our problems with sex are based on a faulty understanding of how human needs are met. We try to meet our spiritual needs in the physical so that we can convince our minds that we are experiencing love. But without that love that originates from within, we're never really satisfied. This is why you still feel lonely even though you are being held. This is why you still feel empty after your escapade. Your spirit is still empty. Still unfulfilled. Still thirsty.

The plan of the enemy is to limit sexuality to the realm of the physical. He wants us to keep trying to quench the spiritual thirst with physical intercourse because the enemy knows how we were made. He knows that the physical can never satisfy the spiritual. When Jesus confronted the woman about her relationship, he was trying to help her realize that she was using her relationship to quench a thirst that would never be quenched by that relationship. Jesus said, "If you drink this water, you will never thirst again". He wanted her to realize that her way of living was standing in the way of the life she wanted. Sex without God satisfies our physical lust. It satisfies our emotional desires. But it can never satisfy our spirit. Only Love can satisfy the spirit. Jesus wanted to make her an offer. He confronted her so that He could quench the thirst of her soul.

Why is sexual purity so important?

Some people ask, "Why do people care about who I'm sleeping with?" It seems like a fair question. Why is purity in sexual expression and monogamy in sexual intercourse so important? I don't believe we are polluted by immoral sexual behavior. We are affected by it but not defiled or polluted by it. The reality is that every sexual expression comes from the deepest and most sacred part of your soul. Sexual sin does not defile you, but it is an indicator that something is missing deep inside of you. Jesus taught this sobering principle in Matthew 15 when he was addressing an issue of Jewish tradition. In Jesus' time, they practiced a ritual of washing hands before eating as a sign of purification. It was not a hygiene issue as much as it was an actual belief that the washing of the hands and eating with clean hands would prevent defilement. While this may have had hygienic value, Jesus knew they had developed a faulty belief around the idea of purity. They believed that what you did with your body and what you put into your body defiled your spirit. But Jesus corrected their understanding by reversing it. He told them this powerful principle. He stated, "It is not what goes into the mouth that defiles a person, but what comes out of the mouth; this defiles a person". This powerful proverb helps us to understand that purity is not simply about what I do with my body, but it has everything to do with who I am on the inside. This goes back to one of our guiding principles. Sexuality comes from our spirit and then goes to our minds, and the body acts it out. In essence, the reason why sexual purity is important is because it is an indication of spiritual health. When our spirit is right, then we make better sexual decisions. It is displayed in our sexuality. We have made a huge mistake in stressing the purity of the body instead of encouraging the purity of the spirit. Spiritual purity comes from being true to your identity and purpose you find in your relationship with God. Every sexual sin begins in the spirit; therefore, the spirit needs to be clean.

This is so simple yet so profound. Sexual purity is actually spiritual purity. If this is true, then this also means that most of us, at varying levels and various times, are sexually impure. Sexual impurity is not about just having lots of sexual partners or cheating on your spouse. If sexual impurity comes from our spirit, then our thoughts, our conversations, and our sexual attitudes are also included. This means that all of us to some extent deal with sexual impurity. This may explain why Jesus, in his classic Sermon on the Mount, talked about adultery in new and challenging ways. He said that the sin was not just cheating on your spouse, but "everyone who looks at a woman with lustful intent has already committed adultery with her in his heart". This means that we all to some extent are susceptible to sexual impurity in us. It begins in our spirit. In our heart of hearts is where the problem lies. And this is why sexual purity is important. It's not because God is trying to stunt your sexual fun. And it's not because God wants us to be boring in the bed. Remember, He created sex. Sexual purity is important because of what it indicates. Something is wrong on the inside when we make bad sexual choices. God cares about the deepest parts of our souls and when we are not spiritually well, it hurts God. Sexual impurity is just an indicator that God's spirit has been limited in your life for some reason. This is why change of behavior only works for a while. This is why change of mindset can help but certainly cannot fix the problem. You have to go deeper. You must go deeper than the wells that you have gone to before to get what you think you've always wanted. Jesus wanted to go to the source of her soul so He could change her from the inside out. And that's what he wants to do for you and me. **God's concern about your purity is not for purity's sake. It's for your spirit's sake.** This is why he came to the well in the first place. He wanted to take this woman deeper. This is why Jesus offered that lady "spring water". He always wants to go deeper. Deeper than the well. Deeper than sexuality. He wanted to change her spirit. Now that's deep.

How do we achieve spiritual purity that will manifest in sexual purity? Spiritual purity comes from having God's spirit in your spirit. While this may sound a bit mystical, the Bible says that God's spirit is in us. Just like the Old Testament Sanctuary had the most holy place, the most holy place of our soul is our spirit. The Holy Spirit, God in Spirit form, desires to live in your human spirit so that the promise of Jesus will be true on your life. Jesus promised that he would send the Holy Spirit so that God could live in you. That is amazing! All of the power of God lives in you. All of the wisdom of God lives in you. All of the resources of God lives in you. This is more than just a spiritual connection or some emotional feeling. Jesus promised us that if we would only make ourselves available, our human souls could house the Spirit of God. This is how our spirit can be purified. We are purified when we let God in us. We cannot clean up our own spirit. We can change our mind. We can also change our behaviors. But spiritual change comes from the Spirit of God and only happens at our spiritual core.

The Woman at the Well was a worshipper of God. When Jesus spoke to her about her lifestyle, she began to talk about her practice of worship. Jesus knew that she did not understand the connection between her sexual relationship and her spiritual state. He knew she thought that she was okay because she worshipped God. However, Jesus makes a radical shift in her perspective. He told her that worship was not about a mountain or temple. It didn't matter where she worshipped God. Jesus told her that worship was not about a place but about a lifestyle. He said, "those who worship God must worship in spirit and truth". He was teaching her that worship must first come from a person's spirit and flow out into everything they do. She could no longer pat herself on the back for worshipping in the right place and then go back to her own private life. Her worship, in truth, was supposed to be infused and enabled by who she really was. No longer could worship be a pretense or façade. She needed her spirit to be filled with the Holy Spirit. When this happened, she would live a true life. A life of love and not regret. A life of peace and not insecurity.

Jesus knew that if He could fill her with His spirit, the rest of her life would be refreshed and redeemed.

How is your spirit doing? Seems like a strange question.

But it is the essential question. We often ask people about how they are doing. We do this in a casual way. But when we understand how we experience life from center to circumference, the question is not about how a person is feeling. The question is 'how is your spirit?' This question is not a question of emotions as much as it is about the condition of your soul. How is your being? It is a question of your state of being.

Are you peaceful?
Are you grateful?
Are you content?
Are you loved well?
Are you safe?
Are you fulfilled?

You need to know the condition of your spirit. **When you know your spirit's condition then you can better understand the decisions you make and the actions you take.** Our actions are the results of our thoughts, and our thoughts are the results of the condition of our spirit. Remember everything flows from center to circumference.

If your spirit is at unrest, you may feel the emotion of sadness. That would cause your shoulders to drop, your face to frown, or your eyes to water with tears. It comes from your spirit to your mind then to your body. If your spirit is disturbed, you may feel the emotion of anger which could cause you to raise your voice, clench your fist, type an angry text, or even punch a wall. It comes from your spirit to your mind then to your body. If your spirit is broken, you may feel depressed which could cause you to sleep excessively, lack energy, and isolate yourself from others. Do you see how this works? So if your spirit is seeking love, you may feel insecure about your worth. This may lead you to dress a certain way for attention. It may lead you to say things you may not say if you felt loved and appreciated. And for many people, this is the reason why they engage in illicit sexual relationships. They mistake their longing to be loved for lust. Lust is not always about the sex we want to have. Lust is often really about the love our souls need. Lust is really our mistaken attempt to satisfy a spiritual need with a physical experience. The spirit feeds the mind, and the body carries it out.

When Jesus asked about her love life, he was really asking about her spiritual state. He already knew how her spirit was doing based on the fact that he knew her sexual lifestyle. You can always tell when a person is not doing well spiritually. It shows in their decisions. It shows up in who they date. It shows in how they relate to people. It shows up in their ability to love and be loved. And it will show in what they will do in order to be loved. Jesus came to deal with her real problem. He wanted to heal her spirit.

THIRST

7

TAKE ME TO CHURCH!

Jesus made a radical shift in understanding the human condition when he referred to the human body as a "temple". This was a radical statement because in Ancient Jewish religious belief and culture, the Temple was the most holy place on earth. The Ark of the Covenant, which held the actual Ten Commandments that God gave to Moses, was contained in the Temple. The precious articles of gold and silver that were mandated by God himself to be used as part of the service in the Temple were housed there. The temple is where the priests of God would intercede on behalf of all the people's sins. It was the place God lived among humanity. So you can only imagine the shock on their faces when Jesus had the audacity to say that His body was the Temple! They were surprised and outraged. This radical statement was really the nail in the coffin for Jesus. Once they heard this, they all wanted to crucify Him. The reason they were so mad was because Jesus was messing with their religion.

Religious people really like systems, rituals, and routines. This shift to "body temples" was an affront to their understanding of their religion. They liked their predictable system partly because they knew what to expect and since it had worked for them all this time, why change it now? But there was a much deeper reason why this statement from Jesus disturbed them. Jesus' statement of the "body as a temple" was the beginning of the dismantling of the compartmentalization of God.

Reverence for the Temple had backfired on the Ancient Israelites. They had come to believe that God only dwelled in the Temple. So in a real sense, they had put God in a box. They had limited God's presence to the holy place of the temple. This allowed them to separate the holy from the secular. This distinction was problematic because it did not allow them to perceive that God's plan was never to be limited to one geographical location. God's plan was to not only be near us or with us, but also to live inside of us. When Jesus pointed to His body and said, "if you destroy this temple, I will raise it back up in three days", he forever changed our concept of who God is and who we really are. Jesus helps us to see that God's intent has always been to live in us.

Everything we do is supposed to be holy. But our religious "boxing in" of God has created a practice of seeing worship as holy and sex as something different. We have adopted this belief that if we are in a church, we are at worship, and if we are having sex, we are doing something far different than worship. If God is regulated to brick and mortar buildings, then we can leave him there while we live our real lives outside of the temple. The teaching of Jesus changed all of this. If we are the Temple, we take the presence of God wherever we go. He is involved in everything we do. There is no distinction between our religious lives and our real lives. We are temples. We were made for God to live in.

Paul took it even further when he helps us to understand that we are "Temples of the Holy Spirit". The apostle Paul taught that when we accept Christ as our Savior, we grant God ownership of our lives. For many people, this is nothing more than a religious experience. But Paul taught that this is not meant to be a religious or belief system. The ownership of God on your life is supposed to be practical. Paul points out that God's authority over our lives includes our body. Our bodies have become the places where God wants to dwell. The most holy place was the part of the temple that God literally lived in. It was God's home on earth. Do you know the word that Paul uses to explain our bodies as temples in 1 Cor. 6? He uses an ancient Greek word, which is translated as "most holy place". Paul was telling us what Jesus was trying to tell the people of His day. Our bodies are now the "most holy place" on earth.

This is a game changing reality. We are not just the Temple, but we are the most holy place! This has profound impact on how we think about our bodies and what we do with our bodies, doesn't it? Think about it. We are where God lives in the earth. God doesn't live in churches, temples, and synagogues. God desires to live in you and me. This means that what I do with my body matters. What I do with my hands is worship. What I do with my legs is worship. What I do in my bedroom is worship too. The radical shift is that God is wherever you and I are. You are the Temple. You don't go to church to meet with God. God is always with you. He is with you at the party. He is with you at the hotel. He is with you at your mistress's place. He is with you as you look at the nude pics on the screen. If we are His Temple, then what we do with our bodies matters. Have you really thought about that? God is in you and what you do with your body matters.

One of the most significant reasons why we struggle with sexual temptation is linked to this reality of our bodies as temples. The enemy of humanity has always wanted to destroy the image of God. However, from the very beginning he has been dedicated to taking over the space where God resides. The Enemy would love to have access to the place where God lives. In fact, think about the fact that the Bible tells us that Satan used to be an angel named Lucifer. He was put out of Heaven due to his desire to take the place of God. He has always wanted to rule the place where God lives. If Satan could not take over the place where God lives in Heaven, you can only imagine how much he wants to take over God's earthly residence in you.

We are the target of Satan's attack because of the presence of God or the potential of God's presence in the life of every human being. When we think of immoral sexual behavior we always focus on the physical act of sex. But you need to know that pre-marital sex or extra-marital sex is not where the real problem is. Remember we are comprised of body, mind, and spirit. Paul really exposes the real challenge when he encourages the Corinthians to "to glorify God in your body and in your spirit, which is the Lord's." Did you catch what he said? He said to honor God in your body and your spirit. Did you notice that we are not just asked to honor God in what we do with our bodies, but also in what happens in our "spirit"? Don't miss the power of that statement. He helps us to understand the real attack is directed toward your spirit. Your spirit is where faith, truth, and virtue reside. If you don't accept the ownership of God in your spirit at any given moment, your mind and body are susceptible to any kind of temptation, including sexual temptation. Our bodies are instruments of our mind and spirit. Whatever is going on in our spirit will manifest in our bodies. Your spirit is what Satan is after. If he can get your spirit, then he can influence your mind and finally your body. If he can attack your faith, your hope, and your sense of worth, then he can alter your thinking. And consequently you will act out in immoral sexuality. But if your spirit can remain strong, your thoughts will be strong, and your body will follow suit. In essence, when we "glorify" God in our spirit, it will be demonstrated in our bodies.

The reason why we want to be pure is because we don't belong to ourselves. He says we are bought with a price. We belong to Jesus because he paid the ultimate price for our bodies, mind and spirit. You are worth so much because of the price paid for you. Don't sell yourself cheap. You are worth more than a one-night stand. You are worth more than a cheap thrill. Men, your masculinity is not based on how many women you can please sexually. Don't sell yourself cheap.

Here is the key to overcoming in this area of body worship. If we are temples that have been created to have God live in us, then the answer to our struggle with sexual sin is the fact that God's spirit desires to live in us. Remember that Satan was kicked out of God's house before. The same God who evicted Satan then is able to do it again in your life. The goal is to allow God's Spirit to live in your spirit. If His Spirit is in your spirit, He can renew your mind to think differently. Then you can do everything that He did!

This is why Jesus told the lady that a time is coming when people will have to worship God in spirit and in truth. Jesus was talking about learning to honor God in and from your spirit. Jesus was offering the lady a revolutionary way of living. No longer would we ask God to come and help us. Jesus was introducing the idea that God desires to come into our lives and give us all His power.

His Spirit in our spirit
His Power in our weakness
His Wisdom in our confusion
His Presence in our messiness

When we have His Spirit, our temples cannot be overrun by Satan. The spiritual principle is this: God's presence and Satan's presence cannot abide in the same place at the same time. Darkness cannot be present where light dwells. So if we let His spirit into our spirit, our minds will be changed. And we will be able to control our sexual activity. You were built for this! You were made to bring glory to God. Let His Spirit into your spirit.

8

SEX AND GUILT

Engaging in something you should not do triggers guilt. Guilt is the mechanism of telling us that we have done something wrong. If we are on a diet and we ate the forbidden doughnuts, we feel guilty. If we were supposed to keep an appointment and we lied to get out if it, we may feel guilty. Somehow, we have convinced ourselves that these feelings will help us do better the next time.

Religion has often used guilt as its weapon to make adherents behave according to the moral code. The idea is that we should feel bad for our mistakes and if we feel bad enough, we will do better. However, feeling bad is not motivation for changing behavior. The power to resist temptation has a lot to do with motivation. If the motivation is negative, the results will be negative. Guilt is simply not wired to accomplish change by itself.

So what is the solution? Maybe we shouldn't feel guilty about anything. Okay. How do we accomplish that? First we can try by normalizing all of our mistakes. Everybody does it so it can't be that bad. If we normalize our behavior then we don't feel so bad about what we are doing because everyone is behaving that way.

Every guy watches porn.
Every teenage girl is having oral sex.
Everybody flirts sometimes.
Every man has to sneak a peek when a woman walks by.

This attempt to normalize our behavior seeks to numb our ability to feel guilty for what we are doing. If we are honest, this doesn't remove guilt. It simply spreads it out and shares it. Our attempts at normalizing guilt simply points out how all of us are flawed human beings. The misery of shared wrong doing only compounds our guilt in the end.

The second tactic we try is to minimize our behavior. In other words, the mistakes we made are not really mistakes or wrongdoing. We may attempt to stop feeling guilty by removing the reality of wrongdoing. But this doesn't work because then how do we determine what remains wrong and what suddenly becomes right? This approach to guilt would be devastating to culture and society on a whole. Although our culture is big on relativism, in reality, there are some things that are not appropriate, and some things that are just plain wrong. We don't escape shame by eradicating guilt. So if we cannot minimize wrongdoing, what can we do?

Some neuroscientists have recently been studying the helpfulness of guilt and have come to the conclusion that guilt is not helpful in changing our behavior. In her book, *The Will Power Instinct,* Dr. Kelli McGonigal, proposes that guilt actually leads to repeating the undesirable action. She argues that guilt sabotages your ability to make a different decision the next time temptation comes around. Based on a few studies, she suggests that guilt hijacks the centers of the brain that deal with self-control. While I find much of Dr. McGonigal's work on the subject of will power to be very helpful, I think we have to consider the fact that she is looking at this subject solely from a scientific perspective. I am one who believes that science and faith are not mutually exclusive. They most often work hand in hand. If we only look at the issue of guilt from a scientific perspective, we miss the spiritual dynamic of guilt. How does guilt relate to our spirit? Can guilt be helpful spiritually?

I agree that guilt is capable of resulting in repeated offenses. However, I believe that outcome only occurs when we allow guilt to lead us into shame. Shame, not guilt, is the biggest trigger for further relapse. Shame actually leads to repeating the undesirable action. Guilt is the awareness that you did something wrong. Shame is the sense that you are wrong. One has to do with the action and the other is the internalization of the wrongdoing. One is helpful, and the other is dangerous. Shame does not help me resist future temptation. All of us have been there. When we feel really bad about something and there is an unhealthy awareness of what we did wrong, we are paralyzed by the reality of our wrong. The feeling of shame seems to freeze or impede our ability to process what steps led up to the mistakes we made. Shame does not allow us to learn from our mistakes. It makes us hide. Shame makes courage leave. Dr. Brene Brown says, "Shame is the intensely painful feeling that we are unworthy of love and belonging". God never intended for us to live in shame because it destroys the ability to experience forgiveness and redemption.

Shame destroys self-esteem and self-value. If people do not value themselves, they have no healthy motivation to make better choices.

McGonigal suggests that if you let yourself off the hook, you can feel better about yourself. Therefore you have the will power to do better next time. I agree that we are too hard on ourselves sometimes, but not in the way she suggests. I don't think guilt has to make us be hard on ourselves. If guilt is the human way of realizing that we have done something wrong, inappropriate or even illegal, then we cannot remove guilt. The question is "Where do we turn after we feel guilty?" What is our response to guilt?

Shame vs. Guilt

If we respond to our guilt with shame, we will feel so terrible about our actions that we are doomed to repeat them. Too many of us choose the shame response to our guilt, and that leads to a very dark path. When we respond to guilt with shame it leads us to condemnation. Condemnation is when I sentence myself to worthlessness and defeat because I have become what I have done. Condemnation is the result of a sense of hopelessness. When we have responded to our guilt with shame, we end up doing something terrible to ourselves. We begin to sentence ourselves to return to the behavior that made us feel guilty in the first place. Why do we do this to ourselves? Why do we repeat the same mistakes after feeling bad about it? The neurological reason would be that our guilty feelings trigger a stress response in our brains that makes us want to do something to alleviate the stress. The spiritual reason is far more significant. When we feel condemned by our own decisions, our spirit is devoid of hope. We tell ourselves that we will never stop. We sentence ourselves to repeat the same behavior because we cannot see how we can be different. Condemnation is always a self-inflicted wound. It is something we do to ourselves.

Guilt can lead to shame.
Shame leads to condemnation.

However, there is another response to guilt. Guilt can be helpful if it leads us to contrition. Contrition is not just simply the awareness of our wrongdoing, but it is also the realization that our actions need to change. Contrition is the most effective response to guilt because it helps to separate us from our actions. Contrition makes you feel sorrow for wrong without the hopelessness. Hope is important. You cannot accomplish any great success without hope. When you are contrite, you understand that you have done something wrong, and you want to change. Contrition can lead to you creating a goal to overcoming the behavior. We call this conviction. Conviction is when you believe that it's worth trying to change. It is a mindset that says that you don't have to live like this anymore. Condemnation leads to despair, but conviction leads to the hope of change. Conviction is the awareness of guilt fueled by the power of hope. Guilt is not the enemy. Your response to guilt determines your ability to overcome the behavior.

God does not work by condemnation. He only works by conviction.

Conviction and Condemnation may sometimes be confusing. But they are different.

Condemnation is the result of shame and leads you to run from God.

God's Response to Your Guilt (Compassion)

The first time we see shame recorded in the Bible is after Adam and Eve's relationship with God has changed. They were naked the entire time, but it isn't until they chose to live life on their own terms do we see their attitude towards their sexuality change. They became ashamed, and their shame caused them to cover up their sexuality. This is no coincidence. The relationship with God was broken, and it altered how they thought about their natural state of being. Their nakedness and all that it implied is now seen as something to be shunned and hidden. And this is what happens whenever we take God out of our relationships. At some point, we become ashamed of who we are.

Shame comes when relationship is broken. Shame is the result of seeing oneself through your own eyes. When

Adam and Eve saw themselves without the trusting relationship with God they had previously, they were ashamed of who they were. This was a critical point in human history. This is when we began to see ourselves through our own eyes instead of through the relationship we had with God. Shame makes you hide. We hide our true selves because we think our partner may not be able to handle who we really are inside. So sexuality and sex becomes clandestine and secret. Before their decision, their reality was defined by God. They had dominion and authority. They had meaning and purpose. But all those things had been granted by their Creator. What they did not fully understand was that they were experiencing the joy of life by way of relationship to their Creator. Their idea of who they were was directly connected to who God was. Their identity was wrapped up in his proximity. When the relationship became different between humanity and divinity, humans began to see themselves and be ashamed. This has affected our sexuality in real ways. Whenever we look at ourselves outside of our relationship with God, we will always find something to be ashamed about.

What was God's original response to human shame? According to Gen. 3, God came looking for them. Usually when you break someone's trust, they leave. But God came. It is customary for people to give up on you once you betray them. But God came. He did not come to condemn them. They had already done that to themselves. Their shame had made them hide and cover up. The miracle is that God came. Shame makes us run away. But God comes. Condemnation makes us hide from everyone. But God still comes. When God showed up, he reminded them of their consequences of their choices. He didn't remove their guilt. He told them the tragic results of their decision. But most of all he showed compassion. How did he show compassion? God came. Not only did he come looking for them, he did something about their shame.

Adam and Eve had made clothes out of fig leaves to cover their shame. Anyone could have seen right through it. They were not sufficient. It was just a feeble attempt to deal with their shame. God did not want them to live in their shame so He made them a coat made from the skin of an animal. He covered their shame with his compassion. He loved them so much that he did something to remove their shame. God wanted to do the same thing for the Woman of Sychar. He knew she had come to the well with great shame. He would not remove her guilt because she needed to acknowledge her life choices. But neither would he let her live in her shame. He offered her compassion. He offered her a new life.

God wants to do the same thing for you. If you are living in shame for your sexual lifestyle, He still shows you compassion. God will turn your shame into contrition and your condemnation into conviction. The key is that you have to exchange your "cover up" for his covering. His compassion will erase your shame and put you on the path of contrition and conviction. It doesn't matter what you have done or are presently doing. Be convicted of this truth: **You are not what you have done. You are who God made you to be.**

9

WHY WE WANT
IT SO BADLY

(ESSENTIALITY AND EXPEDIENCE)

Sex is everywhere and involves everybody. There is nobody on this planet that is not affected by sexuality and sexual expression. It does not matter if you are married, single, straight, gay, man, woman, active or celibate, everyone is involved in sexual expression. This is because to be human is to be sexual. The Catholic priest who takes a vow of celibacy is still sexual because he is vowing to repress a natural urge for a "higher purpose". The person who has convinced themselves that they don't need sexuality is still concerned with it, and if they were honest, they would admit that they still struggle to not think about it. You cannot escape it. So why is sex so important to us?

Sex is basically an appetite. There are at the very least two types of appetite. There are essential appetites. The appetite for food is essential. You need food to live. Food has the nutrients your body needs so that we can function and exist. Water is an essential appetite. We need water for our blood flow and brain function. We need it to replenish the water we use by sweating, talking, and working throughout the day. There are many other essential appetites we have that have nothing to do with our physical existence. These are the spiritual needs we have been talking about. The need to be loved is an essential appetite. Everyone, no matter what they say or how they act, desires to be loved. To be loved is to be fully alive. Without love a person can die, if not physically then spiritually. Essential needs can be defined as "things that would cause you to die if you did not receive them." Everyone needs to satisfy his or her essential appetites. However, the non-essential appetites are different. They are important but not essential. This is a critical difference. Just because something is very important, it may not be essential to one's existence.

We often define what is essential by what is expedient. You see this happen with children. Have you ever wondered why those evil store managers at grocery stores keep putting all that candy at the cash register right at the eye level of your little son or daughter? Do they get some kind of sadistic kick out of watching you have to tell your kid "no" a thousand times? We know why they do it. For the same reason they put all the magazines with half naked women at the cash register. So the little kids can get their candy on the way out and daddy or mommy can get their "fix" on the way out too. They do it to create expedience. Expedience is when you need something, and you need it right now! Expedience cannot wait. Expedience cannot be put off until tomorrow. The temptation of the candy is made expedient by placing it in front of your children so consistently that they convince themselves that they cannot live without it. However, the candy is not an essential part of a kid's diet. It helps to satisfy hunger temporarily, but it is not essential.

This is the same with sexual expression. Sex is not an essential appetite. It is very important and very pleasurable. Sex feels good, and it is good. But sex is not an essential appetite. You can live without having sex. The challenge is that we have made sex expedient to the point that we now believe it is essential. When sex becomes essential, we do whatever it takes to get it. We will cheat, sneak, and creep around to get it. When sex becomes essential, we will make decisions that are not best for us in the long run in order to satisfy a present hunger. Sex has become hyper-important to us because it has been made expedient. We could blame this all on the media and act like they are the culprits. We could lobby Congress and ask for their help to make Internet Porn less accessible to our children. We blame certain musical artists and genres for creating this sexual expedience through their racy lyrics. We could point the finger at the movies and their consistent glamorization of sexual promiscuity. But deep down, we all know that is not the real problem. The "store clerks of sexuality" did not create the expedience by simply putting the candy on the shelf. They put it there because they understand human nature. They know what most kids want. So they simply provide what they want. Free porn sites. Sexually explicit lyrics. Steamy soap operas. They create it because we have made sex expedient. Expedience is not necessarily created. It is simply recognized and exploited.

Let's look at a case study in scripture. There once lived two brothers who were born to Isaac, son of Abraham. Jacob and Esau were twins. Though Esau exited his mother's womb first, his brother Jacob stayed right on his heels literally. The Bible says that when they were born, Jacob came out holding on to Esau's heel as if to say, "Let me out first!" This striving for supremacy would never leave Jacob. Jacob would always want to have the rights and privileges that his older brother had. In the culture of their day, the oldest son was privileged above all other children and ended up with the lion's share of the Father's inheritance. Younger brothers were runners up. Second fiddle. One day Jacob would get the upper hand. He was cooking some lentil stew when Esau came back from a hunting adventure. Esau was hungry. In fact, he was so hungry that he asked Jacob for some of his stew. Jacob sees an opportunity to hold something over his brother. So he proposes that Esau give him his birthright in order to have the food he requested. Now stop right there, and let's take a close look at this. Esau was hungry. Hunger is an appetite. He wanted food, and one could argue that he needed food after being out hunting all day long. But was his hunger essential? The need for food is essential, but the feeling of hunger is not always an indictor of essential need. For instance, my children tell me they are hungry all the time. We could have fed them an hour ago, and they will return with frowned faces and pitiful eyes exclaiming, "I'm hungry!" Just because they express hunger doesn't mean they are hungry enough for it to be essential. Esau might have wanted something to eat, but that's not hunger. Hunger is the need to have an essential need met. Desire is something different. That's when you just want to eat. The funny thing about it is they can feel like the same thing. Our desire can become so strong that we convince ourselves that it is essential. This is the beginning of our troubles with sexual temptation when desire is upgraded to essential need. **When we can no longer tell the difference between desire and essential need, we are in trouble.**

The Bible does not tell us if Esau was unsuccessful in his hunting expedition or not. We could assume that he came back empty-handed, but that may not be the case. He could have had his fresh kills with him. For all we know, he could have had a deer or young buck strapped to his back, ready to be cut, prepared and cooked. If that is the case, we know Esau did not have the patience to wait for what he already had. This would be just like the fiancée that can't wait till wedding night or the husband who travels for work and just needs some sexual release or the young woman who is on the verge of a marriage proposal and sleeps with her man to seal the deal. You have what you are looking for, but you are not willing to wait. Think about it. Esau went hunting for meat and most likely he was successful in getting what he was after. However, because his appetite got the best of him, he actually settles for stew when his goal was to eat meat. Esau forgot the goal and gave into his impulse. The expedient was more important than the goal. Esau was not willing to wait to satisfy his hunger. Esau is so desperate that he literally says, "I'm getting ready to die. Please give me the stew." That was an overstatement if ever there was one. Really Esau? You're gonna die? Really single woman? You're gonna die if you don't receive love from that man? Really young man? You're gonna die if you don't have sex before you turn 21? Really married guy? You're gonna die if you don't add some spice to your sexual experiences? The idea that we will suffer without premarital or extra-marital sex is as ludicrous as Esau stating that his life depended on a bowl of stew! But that's how serious it was for him in that moment. His hunger had become so out of control that he upgraded his desire to one of expedience. He had to have it, and he had to have it immediately. Expedience can be irrational and illogical. He wasn't thinking clearly. He just wanted what he wanted. Sometimes you can want something so bad you make it an expedient need.

Something in Esau made him so irrational that he would even consider giving up what most people would kill for, over a bowl of stew. That something is what drives married men into the arms of strange women in hotel rooms. That something is what makes mothers neglect their children in order to see him again. It is called lust. Lust is what Jacob saw in Esau's eyes. When Jacob saw it, he realized that Esau would do anything to get what he wanted. Did Jacob create this sense of expedience? No, Esau had it in him already. And that's how every sexual temptation begins. It begins with our desire.

We could blame it on music or the Internet, but if the hunger wasn't there, there would be no temptation. The Bible says, "each person is tempted when he is lured and enticed by his own desire"(Jm. 1:14 ESV). We cannot really blame anyone else for our temptation because it comes from within us. It would be helpful if women wore more clothes and if men were not so flirtatious and TV shows weren't so sexually charged, but at the end of the day, if there wasn't any hunger, the ridiculous offer of sexual temptation would not be considered. It's on us, not on them. It's on us because it's in us.

Jacob made the crazy offer while looking into the eyes of a man filled with lust. Esau could almost taste the stew. His salivary glands filled his mouth with anticipatory drool. He doesn't even think about it. He doesn't even hesitate. The lust for food had consumed his rationale, and all he could see is the stew. So he agreed to give up all the power, prestige, and prominence his birthright would give him. And he devours the meal. It is no coincidence that the Bible records Esau finishing the meal hastily and then leaving and hating the fact that he had just given up his birthright. This is the end of lust. It's over so quickly. The euphoria lasts but a few wonderful moments. And when it's over it causes us to end up despising the very thing we had to give up in order to fulfill our expedient desire. So this is why many men act disinterested after having sex with a woman they are dating. Somehow, even men, realize that when we give into sexual desires, we lose something too. We lost control. We lost a part of ourselves. The sex only lasts for a few moments, but those moments change a person's life. When we give into sexual sin, we end up despising the very thing that was precious to us. Our sexual integrity. Once a person despises their own sexual integrity, they will continue to engage freely with other partners. What is lost too easily is often despised greatly. Don't miss the point here. Esau hated something about himself because he gave into temptation. The birthright was not just some inheritance package or their version of a will. The birthright was part of the oldest son's identity. When Esau gave into his own desire, he ended up hating a part of himself! He despised a portion of who he was. Sexual sin makes you despise part of who you are. It makes you doubt who you are in relationship to God. So he walked away from that moment of lustful weakness, leaving a part of who he was behind. Destiny traded in for a bowl of stew. Sex is good. No. Sex is really good. Sex with the right person can be really, really good. Mind-blowing good. Joy-giving good. Worry-taking good. You-forgot-where you-were kinda good. But sex isn't that good. Sex isn't, "lose-the respect-of-your-children" good. Sex is not "I don't care-about-what-the-consequences are" good. Sex is not "give-up-my-dreams and destiny" good. Sex is good, but not that good. We have to think about what we really want in this life.

Andy Stanley gave a message at a Catalyst Conference in 2012 that talked about this story. While his message touched on some different points in the story, he brought great insight to how Esau could have handled this situation better. Andy said that he wished he could have gone back in time to that fateful moment when the offer was made to Esau. He said he would have told Esau that one day his family would grow so large that they would end up in Egypt having been rescued from famine. They would be oppressed by Pharaoh and God would raise up a man named Moses, and he would be their deliverer. Andy said that he would tell Esau that Moses would be approached by God in the wilderness and when Moses asked God his name, God would reply, "I am the God of Abraham, Isaac, and...Esau". We all know that's not what happened. God actually introduces Himself as the God of Abraham, Isaac, and Jacob. Esau might have had the chance to have God call his name if he had made the right choice and kept his birthright. Andy's point was that we should reframe our decisions in relationship to our destiny. How does the momentary decision shape or affect my destiny? How does that illicit rendezvous relate to my future? How does that affair help you with your dream of a happy and whole family? The key to refraining is to refrain long enough so that the strength of the impulse can calm down enough for you to reframe the temptation. If you can just hold out long enough, then you'll have a better chance of being able to center yourself and think about the reality of what you are getting ready to give up for that temptation.

Once we can see further down the road of life, then we can put into perspective that the natural desire for sex before marriage or outside of the boundaries of our marriage is not an essential desire. We can see the stew for what it is. And we can see our future for what it is. We can realize that the trade is not worth it, and we can wait a little longer for our hunger or thirst to be satisfied. You won't die if you have to wait, will you?

The Woman at the Well had settled for being with a man when she was destined for so much more. When Jesus met her, he wanted her to know that she didn't have to sacrifice her essential need in order to get her expedient needs met. Jesus is able to meet both. Jesus wants us to know that the destiny he has for us is not worth trading in for temporary imitations. Why settle for a man when you can have the marriage of your dreams? Why settle for one night when you can have all the nights from this day forward? Why settle for a stolen moment when you can experience love in the open? Jesus helped this lady to know she was destined for so much more. So are you.

10

CHASING YOUR TAIL: THE PROBLEM WITH GETTING WHAT YOU WANT

We once had a dog named Coco. I say we had a dog once because we don't have her anymore. All you dog lovers out there, don't freak out. She is not dead. She's in a better place. Any place other than my house is a better place. She was a cute small puppy that transformed into a huge uncontrollable creature that couldn't fit in our house anymore. So unfortunately, we had to find her a new home. I never had a dog when I was growing up so I didn't know what to expect having a dog as an adult. Coco did this weird thing that I guess many, if not all dogs, do. She chased her tail. She loved chasing her tail, and I always wondered why she did it. We would watch and laugh as she went around and around in a futile attempt to catch her tail. One day, after a couple of minutes of going in circles, Coco actually succeeded in catching her tail. However, when she did, it wasn't the reaction of satisfaction I had expected. She squealed and barked as she realized that when she got what she wanted, she actually hurt herself. She went after the tail and hurt herself.

Sex is so powerful that it creates life. The greatest product of sexual intercourse is human life. This pleasurable process of two people coming together to create a new human being is nothing short of miraculous. **But could it be that if sex can produce life, that it also has the power to destroy life?** Paul says something worth reviewing when he said, "Run from sexual sin! No other sin so clearly affects the body as this one does. For sexual immorality is a sin against your own body." (1 Cor. 6:18 NLT) When we think of sex, we do not usually think of it as self-harm. Sex is pleasurable. Sex feels and is good. But Paul warns us that sexual sin is a form of self-abuse. He is not referring to the physical affects of unprotected sex. Everyone knows that it just makes sense to have protected sex. Sexually transmitted infections and HIV/AIDS are indeed still serious global health threats, but Paul did not suggest "safe sex". He said that sex before or outside of marriage is damaging to the people engaging in sexual activity. Many people who have sex before marriage probably use some form of protection. So why would Paul say that sex can be self-harm?

Sex is binding. What I mean by "binding" is that it is the process of binding or merging two different people together. This is shown in no clearer way than marriage. In almost every marriage ritual, the marriage is consummated or "completed" when the bride and groom engage in sexual intercourse following the wedding ceremony. The two people have been pronounced "one" but they are not really united until the process of sex has made that pronouncement a physical reality. Sex binds the two together. So when you have sex with your partner, you are literally binding yourself to them. You may have just met them last night at the club, but the act of sexual intercourse binds you to that person. You may have just had too many drinks at the office party, and now you are "one" with the girl in the cubicle next to yours. You may have just been curious about what it would be like to have sex with a complete stranger, but now you and that stranger are "one". Sex is binding, but that's not the destructive part. Although when we think of sex that way it can be disturbing. When we have sex outside of marriage, there is no binding commitment to match the binding act we committed to with our body. So when you put your clothes back on and leave that "one night stand" or when you break up with your "friend with benefits", you have just torn apart what you bound through the act of sex. Marital sex binds but premarital and extra-marital sex tears apart. The act of binding is undone with casual sex. You leave that experience torn and the person leaves torn, because the act you engaged in was both a spiritual and physical promise to be bound to each other. This is why Paul said that sexual immorality can harm your body. It tears a part of you every time you engage in the act of binding without making the binding commitment of marriage. This may explain why so many people are left unfulfilled in their romantic relationships. The damage we have done to ourselves by binding ourselves to so many people takes its toll on us. It clouds our ideas of what commitment really is. Our bodies make a lifelong promise that we never intend to keep.

Sexual intercourse outside of marriage not only affects our bodies, but it can have an adverse affect on the most important component of our humanity, our spirit. It is noteworthy, that Paul does not only mention sex in terms of the physical, but also, and more importantly, the spiritual. In 1 Cor. 6:16, Paul says, "Don't you realize that if a man joins himself to a prostitute, he becomes one body with her? For the scriptures say, 'The two are united into one'. But the person who is joined to the Lord is one spirit with him." This reference speaks to the spiritual nature of sex. When we engage in sex outside of the way it was designed to be, we not only bind our bodies to someone, but we bind our spirit to that person's spirit. Both body and spirit are connected through the act of sexuality. The point is that sex brings about a spiritual connection between people that lasts much longer than the sexual experience. It's why you can still think of the person you slept with months ago. You are supposed to think about them. You bonded. It's why you can't get the memory out of your head, even if he wasn't that good in bed. You are supposed to never forget someone you shared your spirit with. It's why you may feel more in love after you had sex than before. You are supposed to feel in love after sex. When you have sex, you always make a spiritual connection.The problem is that you don't just share your spirit with anybody, do you? Sadly, for most people the answer is yes. I am not trying to be mystical here, and neither am I suggesting that we carry around the spirit of every person that we have slept with. When I say that there is a joining of the spirit between you and your sexual partner, I am referring to the spiritual connection that happens in sex that affects your hopes, desires, and vulnerabilities. The spiritual connection happens in two ways.

First, sexual intercourse renders all of us extremely vulnerable. It is designed to help you really see into your partner. There is not only the vulneralibty of nudity, but also it affords you the opportunity to see a person at their worst and best. That is spiritual because it deals with the most delicate and private spaces of any person's life. Secondly, sex connects people spiritually because it allows us to share profoundly deep levels of love, hope, and faith with another human being. Think about it. When you have sex with someone, you are exercising a great level of faith. You are not just letting someone close to you, but you are allowing someone to enter your body. That's exercising faith. At least when you allow the surgeon to operate on you, you are placing your faith in the fact that they went to medical school and practiced this procedure many times before. However when you are having sex, there is not a degree or certificate that can give you some peace of mind that you are in good hands. It is really an act of faith. When you have sex, you are also exercising hope. Sexual intercourse has an innate power to make you hope for a deeper relationship with the person. Regardless of how casual the sex may be, there is a connection that happens deep down that could cause one of you to expect more than just the intercourse. This is natural because sex is supposed to communicate deeper relationship. This is why it's hard to have good sex with someone when the relationship is strained or there is an argument that hasn't been settled. Sex raises expectations that the relationship will go to another level in communication and intimacy. While we know that love can also be communicated during sex, we need to understand that sex can confuse what kind of love we are expressing. When you have sex with someone, the deepest and most important feelings are accessed, and this should only be open to people we know care the deepest about us. Faith, hope and love are spiritual virtues that sex communicates every time we have sex. When we have sex without or outside the spiritual foundation of marriage, the spiritual connection that sex is designed to facilitate is polluted and cheapened.

Sex is meant to produce memories because there has been a spiritual exchange. So how can this be damaging? Think about it. Your spirit is the essence of who you really are. It includes your will, desires, intuition, personality, consciousness of self and the divine. The spirit is what gives us life and makes us human. Your spirit is the best and most important part of you. When you share your spirit with someone through sex, you are sharing the very best and most intimate parts of you. If that connection is made and then severed abruptly over and over again, the damage to who you are can be profound. It changes you. It affects you. It communicates messages to the deepest part of you. One of those messages could be that your worth can be evaluated by people who come in and out of your life. Your self-esteem may become attached to your ability to turn the sexual experience into a relationship. What about the young man who now must measure his masculinity by his sexual performance long before he is mature enough to even know who he really is? What about the young woman who is crushed by the fact that her lover has found another woman to love? We shrug these things off as "lessons learned" or "growing pains". We say to ourselves it's just part of life. We tell ourselves that it's okay and we will get over it. And we do get over it but not without a price. These kinds of pains stay with us simply because they have been imprinted on our hearts through sex. That's what sex is supposed to do. It leaves its spiritual imprint. When I was a kid, my cousin and I were hanging out in the playground of my elementary school playing Tether Ball, when we saw something intriguing to 10 year old boys. It was wet cement. They were pouring a new sidewalk, and they had the area roped off so nobody would disturb it. But we had a bright idea. We knew if we wrote our names in the wet cement before it dried, our names could be forever memorialized in the sidewalk. Everyone would know that we had been there. That's exactly what we did. We imprinted our names in the cement and although weeks and months went by, our names were still there. Sex is like wet cement. It leaves an imprint spiritually. When sex is experienced in a healthy marriage, it imprints on our lives in a positive way. We feel better physically, emotionally, and spiritually. But when it is outside of marriage, it imprints our spirit with doubt, regret, confusion, or even darker realities.

When you are hurt by someone you have had sex with, it always affects you spiritually, sometimes without your consciousness picking it up. Your spirit seems a bit cheapened every time because you allowed another person who was unworthy of sharing your hopes, dreams, fears, and insecurities, into your sacred and most personal space. Would you let anybody into your house? Would you let just anybody walk off the street into your bedroom? Most of us don't like people in our business! So why do we let people into our spirit? Why has sex become an "open door policy" into our most intimate space? The spiritual implications are much far reaching and potentially damaging than an STI or HIV/AIDS. The stakes are much higher when someone's personality, self-image, and future are at stake. Paul was trying to warn us about this. Sex is great. Sex is liberating. It is invigorating. But sex can also damage you in ways that no other experience can. While sex is believed as a way to express one's self-empowerment or liberty from societal restraints, the truth is that when practiced outside of marriage, it is anything but liberty. It is bondage.

11

BAD SEX

(SEX, ABUSE, AND YOUR SPIRIT)

Sex is an experience that simultaneously accesses the three components of humanity: body, mind, and spirit. Sex is not just the coming together of two bodies. It encapsulates all spheres of a person's experience. Some people can have sex without any significant presence of mind. Their bodies are there, but their minds are somewhere else. When two lovers come together, there must be a mental awareness and consent to engage in the experience. The body is obviously engaged in sexuality, but it takes the mental engagement to make it memorable and truly pleasurable. If both body and mind are necessary for sexual experience, then the spirit is also involved on a much deeper level. The spirit is the part of you that truly registers intimacy. It is the part that makes connection and commitment. The spirit is where the stamp of sexuality's promise can be found. When we experience the ultimate human intimacy through sexuality, our mind registers pleasure, but our spirit registers something far deeper. This is why sexual abuse is so damaging. When a person is sexually abused by molestation or rape, there is no consent, and in fact there is protest. The mind is opposed to the experience, and the body reacts to protect itself against the assault. The deeper part of a person's being is accessed through the horrific act of abuse. The body feels the pain, the mind registers the fear and helplessness, and the spirit is hurt because there has been a breach of the deepest part of your intimacy. Hopes are accessed by the monster. Fears are exacerbated as the mind and body have been violated in the worst way. The very essence of who you are has been assaulted completely and simultaneously. This is why rape, molestation, inappropriate touch, and every other kind of sexual abuse is so destructive. It is a triple assault. There are often physical bruises and cuts, but the bruises on the mind and the spirit are far deeper.

If you have suffered this terrible experience, there are no words that anyone could use to explain what you really feel deep in your soul. What I want you to understand is that the shame and pain you feel are a result of your spirit being attacked. There is no coincidence that people who suffer sexual abuse often deal with depression, self-loathing, self-destructive behavior, and hopelessness. It doesn't always happen immediately. Sometimes the mind buries the memories deep down in order to allow the person to forget things that are too ugly and grotesque to remember. All it takes is the right trigger. A failed romantic relationship. A bully who teased you in high school. A moment of quiet reflection. A photo that reminds you of that time in your life. The memories may be a bit hazy, but the emotions that come from that trauma will show up. The feelings of shame and sadness will begin to affect your thinking and eventually your actions. Psychologists and therapists tell us that this is the mind retrieving painful memories. The mind records and stores all of our life's experiences. But there is something else going on in the life of the person who has been assaulted sexually. If the mind stores the memories, I would submit to you that your spirit stores the intentions, hopes, and fears. Sexual abuse is not meant to simply impact the mind negatively, but it is actually done to attack the spirit. As horrible as molestation or rape is, the physical damage is the least of a survivor's worries. The body heals, and the mind may find a way to cope, but the spirit is carrying around the deep spiritual wounds. Proverbs 17:22 says, "A cheerful heart is good medicine, but a broken spirit saps a person's strength". (NLT) The strength you need to overcome the abuse you suffered is not just in your mind. The strength you really need is from your spirit. But when you have a broken spirit, it is hard to move on. Your spirit is where you have the will to live. Your spirit is what helps you get over adversity and push past the pain. However, sexual abuse attacks this very source of your internal strength. Perhaps the reason why you are struggling to heal from the painful past is because you are trying to forget it. But your spirit does not forget. Maybe you have had some counseling, and yet you still can't seem to move past it. Your spirit is still wounded. Somehow you have to address the pain of your broken spirit.

There are signs that we all receive to tell us that our spirit is broken. You know you have a broken spirit when you cannot accept a compliment from the ones you know love you. It's when you feel ugly even if the mirror argues with you. It's when you feel like you never measure up to people's standards. A broken spirit is what makes you seek for love in the all the wrong places. A broken spirit may even cause you to offend others in the same way you were offended and victimized. There is nothing more pitiful than a broken spirit. When you hear of a woman who has been raped or a boy who has been molested, you can bet that their spirits are broken in some way. Their brokenness often contributes to a change in their sexual behavior because if the spirit has been negatively affected it will show up in the way they think about sex and the way they act out sexually. This is not the case for all. We know there are people who have been sexually assaulted, and they are not promiscuous or rigid. However, a great number of survivors are affected by a form of promiscuity or rigidity. Is this your experience? Do you find yourself in sexual escapades more than you would like to mention? Or do you find the very subject repulsive and offensive? Are you grossed out at the thought of sex with your spouse? Or do you have an insatiable desire for intercourse? If you have been abused sexually, this is not abnormal. Neither is it your fault. Your reaction or inability to cope with sexuality is because the core of your sexuality has been shaken. Only the one who gave us our spirit can restore its vitality and strength. The walls of your spirit can be erected once again. You can feel safe again. You can feel whole again. You can be you again.

The healing does not start in the mind. Make no mistake, therapy and counseling are absolutely necessary in the process of healing. I am a firm believer that too many people continue in the hurt and pain because they do not seek the help of a psychotherapist. But in order to be made whole in the mind, body, and spirit, there must be an intervention by the only One who can heal our broken spirit. Let me be clear. God must be allowed to give you back your hope, dreams, personality, and security. Your mind will never be able to accept the truth that you are stronger than your abuse, unless you are willing to accept it. That willingness comes from your spirit. You don't simply think harder or better in order to stir up your will. You have to let that small voice, the voice of God's spirit, convince you that you are worth healing. Your spirit is awakened and encouraged when the One who gave you your spirit is permitted to recalibrate it. Self-worth, self- esteem, and self-image are all restored by a God who helps you to accept his unchanging and undying love for you despite what happened to you. There is one thing you must remember in order for your broken spirit to be made whole. God's love never changes. It does not change based on what you do, and it does not change based on what happened to you. This simple almost childlike statement is so profound that if you can accept this truth, your spirit can be revived. So here it is again. God's love never changes.

Love is the greatest power of all. And if sexual abuse is about power, then sexual healing is about love. "Nothing shall separate us from the love of God which is in Christ Jesus our Lord" (Romans 8:39) Accepting the love of God for you is not just some religious experience that happens at a church building. It happens on the most intimate and personal level of who you are. You must be willing to accept the messages of love that you have received in spite of the abuse. You are still here. You are not a victim but a survivor. Your dreams are still worth pursuing. You did not lose your power because your abuser took advantage of you. This is not easy. I am not in any way trying to be inconsiderate or simplistic. The healing process for the spirit takes time and is hard. But if you don't heal from the inside out, you can never be the "whole" person God intended you to be. The truth of who you are must be accepted in the deepest parts of your hopes and dreams. It is there that the spirit of Jesus puts you back together again.

Jesus said something at the very beginning of his earthly ministry. It was his mission statement so that everyone knew what he was really about. He said, "The Spirit of the Lord is upon me, because he has anointed me to preach the gospel to the poor; he has sent me to heal the broken-hearted, to proclaim liberty to the captives, and recovery of sight to the blind, to set at liberty those who are oppressed." (Luke 4:18 NKJV) When Jesus says, "the broken-hearted" he is talking about the broken spirit. Jesus came to heal your broken spirit. Not just to save humanity. Not just to rescue us from evil. He came to restore the beauty and purity of the human spirit. It is interesting to note other versions of this text do not include the phrase, "he sent me to heal the broken-hearted". In its place, we simply see the next phrase, "to proclaim liberty to the captives". I don't think this is an oversight or mistake by translators. I think proclaiming liberty to captives is related to healing the broken-hearted. They are the same thing. When your heart or spirit is broken, you can become a captive of pain and trauma. You can become a prisoner of your pain. Jesus came to set us free.

The Woman at the Well had been married five times. There is no doubt she was divorced by her husband because a woman could not divorce a man in her culture. She might not have suffered sexual abuse, although it is not out of the realm of possibility based on the low social standing of women in the time that she lived. She may not have suffered abuse, but her heart was broken, and this is why she was in the relationship she was in when she met Jesus. Jesus came to that place that day not to simply receive something but to give her something. He told her that he could give her something that would stop her from needing to come to that Well. While he seemed to be just talking about water, something began to happen in her spirit. She started to have hope. Hope is the cure for a broken spirit. When you can hope for a better future, then you can try again. When you can hope that things will work out, then you can keep going to that counselor's office. When you can hope, you can believe that one day you will be ready to date again or marry again. When you have hope, it helps to initiate your will and your desires. Hope cures the broken spirit. In just mentioning this, he could offer an alternative to her way of life. Jesus gave her hope and that made all the difference in her world. When she hears that she is being offered an alternative, her spirit is revived. If we were there, I think we would have seen her lift her head for the first time in a long time. I can imagine her eyes filled with desire for this water. Hope came to her even though she didn't fully understand what Jesus was offering. Why? Because hope comes to our spirit when we know we have options. Hope comes when we know there is an alternative.

You have options too. You don't have to stay where you are. You don't have to be prisoner to your past pain. There is an alternative. Let the same Jesus who met this Woman give you hope. The hope He can give you is that you don't have to be defined by what happened to you. Neither do you have to be confined by what happened to you. Jesus can heal your spirit with the hope of a new life. He offers a life beyond the memories of your abuse. He offers hope that you can and will move on. The woman began to heal the moment she hoped again. Will you hope again? Hope to be in a loving relationship with someone who doesn't take from you but gives to you. Can you hope again?

THIRST

12

AWKWARD SEX PARTNERS

(THE CHURCH AND SEX)

The Church is still really queasy about sex. This is a strange thing since the Church claims the Holy Scriptures as its foundation of faith. The Bible tells us the story of humanity's origin, which includes human sexuality. So why would the church and sex seem so… awkward? The initial reason would have to be that the Church still has some vestiges of archaic thinking that still influences the way we see and understand sex today. In the early days of the Church, there was a great influence by Greek philosophy and ideas, one of which was the idea that all matter was inherently evil. Flesh was considered something to be abhorred. This translated to anything that brought pleasure. This idea permeated from the Church's theology to its practices. Sex was viewed as a necessary evil in order to produce children. The Church has long since officially abandoned this kind of view. We have come to understand that this view is false. We understand that God created flesh. He called everything he made, "good" and when he made human beings, he called his creation, "very good". The entrance of evil into this world did not change the very nature of flesh. Flesh is not evil because there is evil in the world. Neither is sex evil because it has been corrupted. However, there still remain a few reasons that hinder the Church's ability to communicate about sex.

I think one of the reasons why the Church doesn't like

talking about sex is because sex is too human. It is too real. It is too earthy and natural. While the Christian faith talks a lot about helping people, human relationships, and communal responsibility, it also places a great deal of emphasis on the spiritual and supernatural. For Christians, life really begins far beyond the material world that we live in. The Holy Scriptures calls us to understand that the material and natural does not matter as much as the spiritual and eternal. This idea, though true in so many ways, does not have to cancel out the importance of the natural and material world we live in.

One of the reasons why Christians struggle to fully embrace the beauty and duty of sex is that we are oriented in transcendent thinking when sex is rooted in the here and now. Sex reminds us that we are indeed, at the end of the day, human. Sex reminds us that while we live looking forward to eternity, we live in a natural world that requires attention to our natural needs. This is hard to grasp for so many Christians who believe that a true pursuit of the transcendent is to minimize the duty of the present. Our inability to be real and transparent about our struggles reinforces an idea that we are not supposed to be human. But let's be clear. Spiritual transformation is not the eradication of humanity. It is the perfection of all that it is to be human. In other words, to be spiritually transformed is to be the best human you can be. This includes your sexuality. God intended for us to be the best sexual beings we can be and to have the best sex we can have. Redemption includes everything that is human, including sex.

Another reason for the Church's inability to talk about sex is the idea that due to the human failures of its leaders and membership, the Church is not able to speak with any authority about sexuality. This is an extension of the idea that Christians are superheroes. Somehow we think that

THIRST

our sexual sins and struggles disqualify us because people will think we are "hypocrites". Have you ever stopped to think that maybe it is the way we talk about sex that is the problem? If the Church continues to talk about what is wrong about sex and sexuality today without balancing that conversation with the beauty and multi-faceted purposes of sex, then we will be legitimately viewed as "sex police" and a "holier-than-thou" group of people. Christians need to be honest about our sex lives. The truth is that honesty and transparency never make you look worse. It always reveals the truth of who you are, and the truth of who you are is what helps people to be set free. People need to know that Christians struggle with sexuality just like everybody else. This is not our liability. It is in fact, our asset. The reality is that everyone sees our struggle anyway, so Christians might as well tell the truth. The fear of being called a "hypocrite" is not a valid reason for stepping out of the sexual conversation. Everyone is a hypocrite to some extent. All of us espouse ideals that we don't live up to yet. The difference is when we use our ideals to judge others as unworthy of our love and affection. It's okay for the Church to speak on sexual purity, abstinence, and monogamy, but we cannot do that with one side of our mouth and then cover up our mistakes. The Church has a confession to make. We sin in every way that non-Christians do. That's the truth. So maybe the Church should stop saying "you sinners" and start saying, "we sinners" need God's grace.

Some people don't like to remember their past. The past reminds them of terrible decisions they made. One-night stands that led to months of pain. Hook-ups that led to break ups. Sexual passion turned into heartbreak. The Church struggles with the conversation of sexuality today because church people don't always like to recall their own sexual histories. The inability to look back makes it hard to address the present sexual corruption and degeneration in our world today. It takes a person back to what they have come out of. I have talked to countless Christians who have said that they know that God forgives, but they cannot forgive themselves for the things they did in their past. This lack of self-forgiveness is what makes the Church so silent on these critical issues. This is where the Church needs a dose of its own medicine. If indeed the Christian Church preaches about forgiveness then perhaps the Church needs to learn to forgive itself. The Bible says, "All have sinned and fallen short of God's glory". None of us are perfect. Neither our past mistakes nor our present struggles should silence us about the truth of our human pursuit of spiritual redemption.

The Church Must Speak About Sex

You might wonder why we need the Church to speak up about sex. Don't we hear enough about sex in the media, music, and every kind of communication format? We need the church's voice because we need to hear a different perspective. No society is healthy by simply hearing one perspective on a subject. The Church needs to share why monogamy is an achievable and viable option. The Church needs to share why sexuality should be viewed as sacred and not hedonistic. Society may not always know it, but we need the Church's voice. The problem is not that the Church does not have anything meaningful to add to the conversation on sex. The problem is the church's tone as it relates to sex. The Christian Church has had a lot to say about sex and sexuality in the last decade. The Church has led campaigns against alternative sexual lifestyles. The Church has been vocal on issues of abortion and the choice of a woman. The Church has spoken out against marriage equality efforts. While society may not always agree with the Church's stance on all of these issues, we must realize that Christianity must be able to exercise the same right as every other group or organization in this country. The right to freedom of speech and thought is the right of everyone. The problem I have with the Church is our tone. We sound so hateful. We seem so angry. Where is all the rage coming from? Why can't the Church share its views without being so condescending and judgmental? The Church has to learn how to change its tone in sharing biblical truth and principles. Sometimes it's not what you say but how you say it. I think the Church has been saying it wrong. We are told to "speak the truth in love".

The truth is that the Church has not always been "loving" about its views on sexuality. This negative tone has caused the message to be lost in translation. While I believe that the Church's biblical message of sexuality will never be popular, we cannot blame its lack of acceptance solely on cultural hedonism. Could it be that a few more people may listen if our tone was loving and not hateful? What if our tone communicated genuine concern instead of polite tolerance of an opposing view? What if we actually stopped yelling our opinions and started a real conversation? I'm not being simplistic. I know that there are groups of people who wholeheartedly reject the validity of any biblical worldview. I am aware that many people don't even want to hear the Church's voice. But this cannot be used as an excuse. The Church, if they are led by Christ, must be held to a much higher standard. The tone is as important as the message.

The Church must begin to talk about sexuality not only by changing the tone but by speaking in a different way. The Church has talked too much without truly communicating its message. Let me explain. Most people don't want to hear another sermon about some Biblical ideal. They want to see it lived out in practical ways. The Church has been preaching something it has not always been practicing. The whole idea about sex has to be approached in a different way, if the Church is going to be a viable voice in the conversation about sex.

One of the greatest enemies to the message of monogamy is the rate of infidelity in the Church. Why would I want to listen to a group of people who espouse one thing and practice the opposite? The Church talks about marriage between a man and a woman, and yet the rate of divorce among heterosexual Christian couples is the same as those outside the Church. The Christian Church needs to speak out more on these crucial issues. There are two ways the Church will need to do this:

1. Example
The proof that we actually have a viable message about sexuality is not in how loud and vigorously we can protest today's sexual depravity. The only chance for the Church to be a part of the ongoing conversation on sex and sexuality is to begin to set an example in our sexuality. We do not have to be blameless and perfect, but if indeed God is doing something transformative in our lives, it should be evident in some real and tangible way. Jesus said, "Let them see your good works and they will glorify your Father which is in Heaven". Our good works are God's best marketing tool to share His message with the world. People will not believe us if they cannot see that monogamy works. There is no validity to the Church's biblical message if we don't stop covering up sexual abuse in the Church. Our words are not what matter right now. What matters most is how we live. If we are not at least struggling to live what we preach, then perhaps they should not believe a word we say.

2. Empathy
We all deal with sexual temptations and sin. Therefore, Christians need to be more empathetic. The reality is that empathy should be our default. Arrogance or delusion blinds so many Christians to the fact that they are guilty of the same sins they point out in other people's lives. If the Church would stop seeking to be understood and seek

to understand then we would be in a position to partner with people to deal with their issues because their issues are our issues. When people feel like you understand them, they are willing to share and hear what you have to say. Empathy is the most important way the Church will regain their seat at the table of ideas in the culture. Our shared humanity is what we must recognize. Our common recognition of our humanity is what builds bridges of trust. The Church is made of flawed, finite people. The Church has to look in the mirror and recognize that we are just as human as everyone else.

Sex Abuse in the Church

The Church has a strange silence about sexual abuse. We know it is wrong. We understand its destructive power in the lives of its victims. The church has a well-earned reputation for covering up for its predatory leaders and doing too little to hold victimizers accountable for their actions. I have always wondered why the Church is so silent on the issue of abuse until I became a pastor. I have come across a few situations where I have had to deal with sexual abuse or sexual harassment in my congregation. One of the things that makes reporting and dealing with sexual abuse in the Church so difficult is that there is sometimes a naivety to the reality that the Church is full of people with all types of issues, including sex offenders. This naivety leads to an inability to believe when reports are made. The Church cannot continue to let its leaders and members who offend get away with ruining people's lives. While the Christian Church has been known for speaking out against sexual immorality in the culture, it is tragically ironic that they have been silent on issues that Jesus was loud about and loud on issues Jesus never directly addressed. The Bible records Jesus' statement about how he feels about those who hurt or offend young children. Jesus said, "it would be better for a person to tie a milestone around his neck and throw himself in the sea than to hurt one of these little ones". While this does not mean Jesus wanted people to commit suicide, it does communicate that He thought child abuse of all kinds including sexual abuse was vile and absolutely intolerable. How come the Church does not make such strong statements about sexuality in the realm of sexual abuse? I rarely if ever hear evangelicals running campaigns to stop the proliferation of rape and sexual offenses on college campuses where these sorts of crimes are on the rise. What about the Church's efforts to support rape victims? Why does the Church spend so much time on one area of sexual immorality rather than others?

While in college, my wife was talking with a group of young ladies from her local church about sexuality and relationships. The discussion topic turned to sexual abuse, and 8 of the 10 women who were in that group had been molested in their childhood either by a family member or church member. That's 80%. People of faith cannot afford to ignore this. The silence must be broken. I would rather the Church err on the side of being overly cautious than underestimating the reality of this problem. The damage to so many lives is unthinkable and intolerable. If the Church truly understands that sex is one of the gifts of God to humanity, then we should be the first ones protecting its sanctity by protecting the innocent, defenseless, and the victimized. The voice of the Church on issues of sexuality in the culture cannot be heard or respected when it does not address the sexual abuses of its members and leaders. If the Church is going to lead in the redemption of sex and sexuality it must do so in a role of advocacy. Jesus always spoke on behalf of the abused and the oppressed. Will the Church do the same as Jesus?

The fact that Jesus was talking to this woman was revolutionary. He shows us how the Christian Church should approach the topic of sexuality in society. He wasn't yelling. He wasn't condescending. He wasn't judgmental. He spoke the truth in love.

He spoke the truth. "The one you are with now is not your husband"

He said it with love. No anger. No picket signs. No angry shouts.

He didn't shy away from the difficult topic and neither did he back away from the truth. He was truthful and loving. And the woman didn't run away. She didn't tune him out. In fact, she leaned in to discuss more. Even though this man had confronted her about her lifestyle, He did it in such a way that she was intrigued and not repulsed. Jesus was not intimidated by her sexual sin. If Jesus is not repulsed, and He's the Son of God, I don't understand why the Church is so angry. He simply stayed there with her and talked. He is the same today. He is not repulsed by our sexual sin. He is not angry with us for our choices. He simply tells us that if we would choose what He has to offer, we would be much happier. I wish the Church would be more like its Leader. I wish the Church could be more like Jesus when it comes to sex.

13

PHARISEE IN THE STREET BUT A FREAK IN THE BED

When the Church actually talks about sex and sexuality, it is often represented by groups that seem judgmental and self-righteous. Some of these groups are either self-identified or viewed as "Conservatives". I am not using this term in a derogatory sense. Neither am I using it in a political sense. Conservatives in the church are those who are viewed as the "moral police". They are the people who are always worried about what other people are doing. They want to make sure everyone is following the rules. They are always concerned with orthodoxy and uniformity in behavior. While there is nothing wrong with morality, these people are more concerned with morality than they are with love. In the time of Jesus, there was a group of people who had the same approach to religion. They were called Pharisees. They were highly respected for their knowledge of the Law. They were the ones who helped the Jews to interpret the Laws of the Torah, and they held incredible power over the way the Law was applied to people's daily lives. The Pharisees had power and prestige. But like most people who have access to this kind of power, there were many who had become corrupt. Their unchecked power caused many of them to feel as if they were above the law that they held everyone else to obey. So the Pharisees were publicly known for their law keeping, but Jesus exposed them to be a group of hypocrites. Many conservatives are modern day Pharisees. They know the rules, and they make sure you keep them.

The signature challenge that faces people like this is not simply the fact that they are so rigid and strict. There are many people who live strict and controlled lives, and they are highly productive. They may not be the life of any party, but they don't bother anybody either. The problem is not with strictness. The problem is why Pharisees are so strict. Pharisees believe they have to be strict, rigid, and judgmental in order to earn their worthiness to be loved by God. They will never admit it, but it is their underlying understanding of how to relate to God. They are behavior-oriented. God must be pleased with my actions in order to love, accept and use me. This is the thinking of a Pharisee. They have a fear-based version of religion, and fear is not sustainable motivation for morality. Fear eventually wears off. When the natural human temptation of sexual expression is presented, fear of God cannot and will not protect you. This is what the Pharisee does not understand. So the Pharisee will fall to sexual temptation just like anyone else, but because they specialize in telling everyone else what to do, they try to keep up the appearance that they are keeping all the rules. They will often be more adamant about the rules, all the while they are breaking the very rules they are advocating for. Their motivation for morality was wrong; therefore, the power to live morally is critically compromised. I have never met a strict, rigid, judgmental, behavior-oriented religious person that did not have a problem with sexuality or sexual expression. Never. It seems like the more "judgmental" they are, the more scandalous their past. Strictness simply for the sake of appearances or earning God's love, always leads to breaking the very rules you are trying to keep. The very nature of the "behavior" orientation to religion leads to sexual sin.

The reason why Pharisees are so "anti-sexual" is because they are fighting a fierce internal struggle with the same demons. The veracity with which they attack people is only matched by the internal conflict they face everyday. It is overcompensation in order to camouflage what they are going through themselves. They believe that they can clean their guilty conscience by "making it up" to God. They swing from hypersexuality to anti-sexuality. This is a futile attempt at self-cleansing that only ends up in personal frustration and failure. Maybe that's you. Maybe you find yourself trying to make up for the mistakes you've made. Maybe you are the wife who had some sexual partners before you got married, and due to your shame from what you've done, you are sexually rigid. Maybe you are the man who sowed too many "wild oats" and you're afraid that your actions will catch up with you so you are afraid of sexuality. Maybe you are the person who lives a life of guilt to the point that you cannot experience joy. Let me liberate you. You don't have to live that way. You can live in the joy and gratefulness of forgiveness.

People who are rigidly conservative often mean well but misunderstand what grace is. We all deal with sexual temptation and sexual sin. We just have to be reminded that we are all on the same level no matter if our actions may be different. In John 8, there is the story of a woman who was caught in the very act of adultery. This begs the question, "How did they catch her "in the act"? Was it a sting operation? And what happened to the guy who was with her? How come he wasn't caught? Well, all we know is that she was caught. Guess who caught her? That's right. The Pharisees. They drag her before Jesus and tell Jesus what the Law states about anyone caught in adultery. This woman deserved to be stoned to death. Jesus knelt down in the sand and began to write. We are not told what he wrote, but I suspect that it caught the attention of the Pharisees. He stood up and said, "Let the one who

THIRST

has never sinned throw the first stone." Then he knelt back down in the sand and continued writing. All the Pharisees dropped their stones of judgment and walked away. Not one stone was thrown. What do you think Jesus wrote in the sand that day? I think he wrote the details of their own sexual sins. How do I know? Well, the Law only prescribed stoning for certain sins. If their sins had been of a "lesser" nature, they could have still judged themselves better than the woman and stoned her. But I suspect the reason that they could not stone her was because they had, at some point, done the very same thing that she did and were never caught. They didn't stone her because to stone her was to stone themselves. All of us have a bit of Pharisee in us. We see other people's sexual behavior and we judge them, but we are guilty in some other sexual sin, even if it is simply fantasizing about what we wish we could do. Maybe we should all look at what Jesus wrote in the sand. Maybe if we see our mistakes written there, we will stop throwing stones and accept the forgiveness that precious woman received that day.

When the Woman at the Well came into contact with Jesus, she was definitely guilty of living a life that was dishonorable. When Jesus mentioned her relationship, she had been caught and exposed. But Jesus did not humiliate her. Neither did He judge her. Jesus was a Rabbi, so it was his obligation to execute judgment on her for her lifestyle, but he would not. The Woman at the Well deserved punishment for her sin, but Jesus offered her a new kind of life. He did not prescribe a new pattern of behavior. He didn't tell her to act in a different way. Jesus offered her something that would cleanse her from the inside out so that she would be free to live a better life in peace. Conservatives are into behavior change, but Jesus offers us spirit change. One lasts for a while, but the other last forever. One requires a lot of work from us, but the other requires Jesus doing all the work. He said to her, "If you only knew the gift of God and who it is that is speaking to you, you would have asked him, and he would have given you living water". Jesus still says the same thing to every person who is trying so hard to change their own lives. He is saying, "If you only knew who I was, you would stop trying harder to make up for your mistakes and start asking for the grace I can give." Jesus does not require outward change without first giving you an internal one. The power is not what you do, but what is inside you. Jesus is still making the offer. If you only knew how much grace is available to you!

14

CASUAL

The prevailing idea is that women have sex based on emotions, and men have sex to satisfy a physiological need. We see it in movies and hear it in songs all the time. Women have sex for love or to secure love while men have sex to simply release tension, show their manhood, or dominate the woman in some way. I have a problem with this idea. This thinking renders men as nothing more than sex-driven creatures that cannot help themselves and women as "lovesick" puppies roaming around looking for men who will take them in and show them some love. It minimizes the complexity of our humanity. I think both men and women use sex for similar reasons. Our reasons for having sex and expressing our sexuality are based on the needs that all human beings have: love, acceptance, security, approval, and unity.

Though it can be said that women and men may approach sex differently, we approach it for the same reasons. Men have sex because they are looking for love too. Men are also looking for acceptance. Men are looking for validation Men need the affirmation that sexual intercourse brings. Women aren't just hopeless romantics. Women are looking for the same approval men are looking for. They want to be valued and acknowledged. Sexual intercourse is often what we use in order to get these existential needs met. The challenge is that the sexual act is only part of the experience that satisfies these existential needs.

Acceptance, admiration, and validation are best communicated and received in the context of love. And not all sex happens in the context of love. Men leave sexual hook-ups just as empty as women do. Women aren't the only ones who are not satisfied by sexual promiscuity. The difference may be that the culture we live in celebrates a sexually explicit male and still shuns the woman for the same behavior. The point here is that while men and women may approach sex differently, both seek to get the same things from it. Our sexual needs are essentially spiritual. Therefore, sex is never casual.

One of the most popular songs to hit the airwaves in 2014 was a song called "Stay With Me" from UK soul singer Sam Smith. In the song, Sam sings,

"Guess, it's true I'm not good at a one-night stand,
but I still need love 'cause I'm just a man,
these nights never seem to go to plan,
I don't want you to leave, will you hold my hand"

Smith finally gives voice to what really happens during hook ups and one-night-stands. Everyone leaves without what they really need. He expresses the truth of what every man truly needs, regardless of sexual experience, prowess, or orientation. Love is what every man is seeking even if he doesn't know it. But love doesn't just happen and certainly doesn't happen in a night. The truth is that sexual intercourse for the sake of having sex just doesn't work. Like Sam said, "these nights never seem to go to plan." You planned on having a good time, but sometime later you end up unfulfilled. Even if the one night turns into a few nights, the truth is that the security and love your spirit longs for is not satisfied. Sam goes on to plead:

"Stay with me, 'cause you're all I need,
This ain't love it's plain to see, but darling stay with me"

It really speaks to this man's need for security. But what he doesn't understand is that his lover is not all he needs. He admits that he knows that the relationship is not about love and that alone creates a sense of insecurity. He pleads for his lover to stay and sleep with him so he can feel secure, but that security he seeks is not based in love. Therefore, he knows it won't last. This song helps us to understand the insanity of casual sex.

One of the reasons why one-night-stands don't work is that while the act of sexual intercourse communicates security, it cannot deliver what it promises because you barely know the person you are sleeping with. You do not even know if the person is really safe, not to mention worth making love to them. You don't know what kind of person she or he may be. Let's take an example of someone you may be dating. You could say that you know them pretty well. Perhaps you could say that since you love each other, sexual intercourse is the next natural step in order to communicate that love. But remember, sex promises eternity. Sex connects you spiritually. What happens if that relationship ends? There was never a promise of eternal love with the person you were dating; yet, sexual intercourse communicates that reality whether we mean to communicate that or not. While sex may make us feel secure at the time, we can actually leave feeling more insecure. That's why you feel bad if he or she sleeps with someone else even though you may not be "officially" dating. That's why you often feel something strange down in your chest when you see them with someone else. You don't feel secure. The very thing that sex was meant to communicate is undermined by the one-night-stand experience because you can't be secure with someone you really don't know. What Sam didn't really understand is that if his lover stayed with him, he still would feel alone. Why? If there is no exclusive, committed love that is rooted in God's original design, then sexual intercourse cannot deliver what we desire.

The Problem with Porn

The issue has been discussed in many circles, and the summary is the same: porn is bad for you. Someone may say that porn is only bad for you if you watch it secretly or consistently. But may I suggest to you that it's not what your eyes are seeing that is the worst part of porn. It is what your spirit is receiving. Porn robs sexuality of its most essential component, which is love. It not only objectifies the man and woman to solely sexual beings, but it objectifies sex as something separate and distinct from love. Porn is actually an escape, but not simply a sexual escape into fantasy (since most people cannot do what porn stars do). It is more of an escape from love. When you think about it, porn is the easy way out. When you immerse yourself in porn, you don't have to "feel." You are not required to love. You are not responsible or accountable to each other. Porn eliminates the need for love. This is why it's so damaging.

We all need love. We were created for love. So if you take the "loving" out of love, all you have is an empty act. Maybe this is why porn is so addictive. It's like empty calories. It feels good while you are involved in it, but after it's over, you are still hungry. Porn exacerbates an unquenchable thirst that it can never completely satisfy. This is much like what Jesus said to the Woman at the Well. He told her that if she kept coming to that well looking for something to quench her inner thirst, she would remain thirsty. But He offered her something that would quench her greatest thirst. He offered her love. You cannot quench a spiritual thirst with physical water. And you cannot quench your true sexual desire with porn. Why? Because true sexual desire is essentially spiritual. Sexual desire comes from spiritual desire. We learn from this woman at the Well that no matter how many people you sleep with or how many times you get married, the need for unconditional love will always be there. You will never be satisfied until your soul is satisfied. The deepest part of you is your spirit. That's a place nobody else can touch but God.

Everybody Loves Porn

In 1 Cor. 5:1, the word fornication is used from the KJV of the Bible. But the term in the original language is "porneia," which means sexual immorality. This word is really close to a word we know. The word porneia relates to sexual intercourse outside of marriage, either before marriage or outside of the marriage boundaries. According to the Bible, sex outside of marriage is called "porn." When we think of porn, we think of racy videos, naked pics, and internet sites. However, the word porn relates to every kind of sexual act outside from God's original design. Porneia is sexual intercourse outside God's will. Porneia is sex before marriage. Porneia is sex with other people while you are married. Porneia is homosexuality. Porneia is engaging in B&D. Porneia is even sex with a woman who is not divorced for biblical reasons. (Mark 10:11-12)

Some people will judge people who are actively watching and buying porn videos and reading pornographic material. But the truth is, so many church people are engaged in porn without ever watching a dirty video or viewing naked pics. Porn is not as narrow as we think. Jesus comes and narrows the definition by including our thought patterns. Porn is everyone's problem. It is a cheap version of the beautiful original. Porn makes the sacred, casual.

Sex is for marriage. The human need for love, security and unity that both men and women have can be met uniquely within the environment of marriage. The most unique feature of marriage that makes sexual intercourse most meaningful is the fact that marriage was meant to last a lifetime. But since an alarming percentage of marriages today are ending in divorce, we must ask ourselves the question. "Does sex still have the significance it was meant to have since marriage seems to have lost its significance?" I think the answer is still "yes." While people give up on their own marriages, it doesn't mean that marriage is no longer a meaningful commitment. The issue is not that the marriage institution has lost its significance but that the culture does not value commitment and endurance, and that is having its effect on married couples. Sexual expression cannot be ripped away from marriage simply because we are not as committed to marriage anymore. Perhaps the rising divorce rates have more to do with human selfishness and greed than anything else.

Marriages aren't lasting because selfishness is much more pervasive and acceptable in our culture today. This "me-before-everybody-else" culture has made the thought of committing to someone else seem unbearable. But this does not mean that marriage doesn't work anymore than saying we should not commit to nutrition and exercise because most people cannot stay committed to eating right and exercise. Marriage still matters and marital sex is still the best sex. The most definitive and important component of marital sex is the promise and pursuit of agape love. That is what keeps two people together no matter what may happen to them. Sex in marriage is one of the ways people show their agape for one another. When they make love in the atmosphere of agape, they feel more secure and more loved. Marriage is not perfect, far from it. But it is the place of love that allows us to be vulnerable and yet validated. It is the place where we can be honest and still feel secure. In marriage, we make a promise to stay no matter what. Marriage is the way we receive everything Sam Smith was wanting.

The Woman at the Well had given up on marriage. She had fallen into the causal sex zone. Jesus knew this and that's why he explained her relationship as, "the one you are with now." That had a particularly casual feel to it. No commitment. No drama. No satisfaction either. She had given up on committed love and settled for causal relationship. Jesus wanted her to understand that she did not have to settle for a casual, fleeting experience. He came to let her know that she was worth committed love. In fact, she did not know that she was talking to Committed Love in the flesh. She had not known what it was to be loved with commitment. After all, she had been divorced by five different men, so how could she believe in love? Jesus wanted her to know that love had come to her at the Well that day. Love has already come for you too. Why settle for a casual relationship when you can wait for commitment? When you wait, you are not promised that you will ever receive committed love by getting married. However, you will experience the peace that comes from knowing you are not settling for a relationship that will only make you feel more insecure. The Woman at the Well began to realize that her casual relationship was not as satisfying as she might have thought.

15

THE TRUE NATURE OF TEMPTATION

Our temptation is never really about what it seems. Sexual temptation is not about just wanting to have sex. It's really about something far deeper and far greater. Sexual temptation begins in a person's spirit. Remember, every action moves from center to circumference, from the inside out. We see this in the temptation of Jesus in the desert. In Matt. 4:3-11, we read the account of Jesus' temptation. The Devil comes to Jesus after He is hungry and tired and he says, "If you are the Son of God, turn these stones into bread…," and Jesus is able to resist. At first glance, it seems as if the Devil is tempting Jesus to use his power to turn stones into bread, but that is not the temptation here. Notice how the Devil begins his temptation. When the Devil asks, "If you are the Son of God…," he actually is tempting Jesus to question who He really is. The temptation is not about His ability but about His identity. Every temptation begins with identity. Identity has to do with who you really are in the innermost part of your soul. If you doubt who you are or don't know who you are, then you are susceptible to using your ability to satisfy your appetites and desires. Jesus' identity was not just tied to His birthplace in Bethlehem or His upbringing in Nazareth. His identity related to His purpose. When the Devil used the term "Son of God" he was referring to both Jesus' identity and purpose. Jesus was the Son of God by origin because He came from God as He said in John 1. But he was also the unique Son of God by purpose because as the Son of God, He came for the expressed purpose of dying for humanity's sins and revealing the character of God to a race of human beings who had forgotten how wonderful God is. Simply put, his identity and purpose were one and the same. Because he knew who He was and why He was, Jesus was able to withstand the temptation. Your understanding of who you are and what you are called to be has a lot to do with your ability to resist temptation.

Identity and Temptation

I live in Atlanta where there is a ridiculous amount of sex trafficking going on. Young girls are "pimped out" by both domestic and international human traffickers. Many young girls are brought in from international locations to Atlanta because the city has strategically become an intersection for travel and commerce. It is a sad situation that the church, government, and the private sector need to collaborate to address and eradicate. There are the girls that ended up in the sex trade because they ran away from home. Some of them were running from abuse. Others ran away from neglect. They left because they felt overlooked and underappreciated. They were not valued or loved. They were susceptible because they were hungry for all the things young ladies need. However, their greatest susceptibility was that they did not understand who they were. When your home is in chaos, and the ones who are supposed to love you and make you feel secure do not provide you with the very basics of human development, it robs you of your opportunity to really know who you are. When you don't know who you are, anybody can tell you who you are. When you don't have an identity, someone can come along and assign you one. For many of these teenage girls, they have been given their identity as sex objects. They are told they are pretty, and that becomes their identity. They are told they are sexy, and that becomes their identity. Once their identity has been reduced to the realm of sexuality, they are easily wooed into living out their sad new identity.

Identity is the property of the human spirit. We do not simply know our identity mentally or physically, but our identity is essentially realized in our spirit. Our real identity is who we truly believe we are to our core and not simply what creed we subscribe to. Jesus never asked the Woman at the Well about her identity. He never asked her for her name. I think he didn't have to ask for her name because he knew she didn't really know who she was anyway. Notice that while he never asked her for her name, he did ask to meet her husband. He knew she wasn't married but that wasn't his real reason for asking about her husband. Jesus wanted to address her lifestyle because her lifestyle was telling Him more about her identity than any name ever could.

Christ's acceptance of his spiritual identity empowered him to say no, when his body begged him to say yes. Once there was a King named David. He was the beloved King of Israel. The Bible records in 2 Sam. 11, King David stayed home during the time that kings would usually go home or go out. One late afternoon he walked out on his balcony only to see a beautiful woman named Bathsheba bathing. He sent for her and when she came to the palace, he slept with her. In this example, we see the connection between purpose and temptation. David was not living in his purpose at the time. This was not just a case of being idle or bored. David was obviously not living in His purpose. He had sent an underling to do what only a King should do. When we are off-purpose, we are susceptible to sexual temptation. Purpose keeps us focused on the things that matter the most. Purpose helps us to use our power for the right things. David used his power to bring Bathsheba to his bed. His authority that should have been used to command troops and execute military strategy was used to command a woman to fill his bed. That is not only an abuse of power - it is an abuse of purpose. Jesus' purpose was challenged in his temptation. The temptation was not just about turning stones in to bread, but it was also about using his power, like King David did, in order to satisfy himself. The temptation was to waste His purpose on stones and bread. The Bible teaches us that our purpose is to live for love and Love is God. Our purpose is to be loved by God and to show His love to others. This purpose guides and guards our decisions. Purpose guards you from distractions and guides you around diversions. Kind David forgot his purpose and became distracted by another man's wife. Isn't it true that when you get off purpose that you notice temptations that you just don't notice when you are "in the zone"?

Basketball players talk about how they are able to block out the screams, heckling and waving arms of the opposing team's fans during a game. When asked how they do it, the only way they can describe it is that they go into an extreme focus where they are able to ignore all the noise and distractions. They focus on creating a play, getting the ball down the court, setting up a shot and executing the plan. They focus on winning. They call it "the zone." The zone mindset is based on the player remembering their purpose. Purpose is what causes them to put all the external stimuli into perspective. When they are committed to their purpose, they can even play through injuries and sickness because purpose doesn't let you go until you fulfill it. King David was not in the zone that afternoon. He was paying attention to something that had nothing to do with leading the nation, keeping his people safe, or governing the land. In fact, because he was not in the purpose zone, he put his armies at risk and ended up killing Bathsheba's husband just to have her for himself. Sexual temptation often overtakes us when we are out of our Purpose zone. We see things in people that if we were in the zone, we would never see. I've talked with people who looked back on the people they hooked up with and wondered what they were thinking. In retrospect, it was at a time when they were searching for purpose or had lost sight of their purpose.

When you understand your purpose, it helps you to make decisions that will not derail your own dreams. When you understand that you have a critical contribution to make to society, you think twice about your sexual decisions. In Jesus' case, bread was not just a desire, it was a necessity. His body craved for it. But his sense of identity and purpose overrode his need to satisfy his body. He was able to say "no" because he had already said "yes" to something far greater. Jesus had just been baptized. When he was baptized, something remarkable happened. The gospel writer records that God the Father spoke from Heaven and said in an audible voice, "This is my Son in whom I am well pleased." God wanted everyone to know Jesus' true identity, the unique and chosen Son of God. But I also believe he wanted Jesus to be reassured in his identity. Once Jesus received this commendation from His heavenly Father he was ready for the temptation. He went into the desert knowing who He was and what His purpose was. This is why he was able to overcome the temptation. Even if your body wants it, your spirit reminds your mind who you are and what you're about. When you know who you are and what you are here for, the battle is won. When you know in your spirit that you are inherently special, precious, wonderful, and valuable, then you can formulate a healthy identity. The need to truly know and accept your value is priceless. If a young woman knows she is precious, it doesn't matter what is said to her or presented to her, she can say no because she knows who she is. When a young man knows who he is, he will not give into that internal notion that he has to prove himself sexually in order to be accepted by the culture. There's one more thing about this temptation of Jesus. He had been in this desert for 40 days, and no doubt he was near the end of his time there. His temptation came just before he would get out of the desert. He was just about to begin his ministry on the other side of the desert. His purpose was about to be fully realized. After His temptation, he began to preach the gospel, heal diseases, and change people's lives. Sometimes our greatest temptations come just before we are about to go to the next level of our purpose. So hold on to what you know about who you are and what you are called to do. Your greatest successes in life are preceded by your greatest temptations.

According to Kelli McGonigal, self-control requires the brain to use more energy than almost anything else it does. It is hard to say no. This is why spiritual strength that is rooted in knowing who you are in relationship to your God given purpose is important. Your spirit is what gives you the will power to convince your mind that it is worth resisting. In a real sense, knowing who you are and your purpose is the key to self-control in the midst of any type of temptation including sexual temptation.

Jesus knew this Woman at the Well didn't know who she was. Her scandalous relationship was proof of her uncertainty. But Jesus had come to let her know her identity and purpose. She was not what she had done. She could not be defined by her actions. Jesus told her that she was destined to be internally satisfied. Her identity was "child of God." Her purpose was to be revealed very soon. But before she could embrace her purpose, she had to accept who she was to God.

Do you know who you are to God? Do you understand how important you are to Jesus? You need to know that you are not defined by what you do. You are defined by the love that created you. You are here for a purpose. You are here to be loved. And please know this, you are loved. You are loved by a God whose whisper can be heard in the rhythm of your heartbeat. You can sense His love in the mercy that is shown everyday that you are given another chance to wake up and experience life another day. You need to know who you are. You are not what you have done. You are God's child. You are the object of His perfect affection. You have to accept who you are to God. Be loved by him so that your identity will no longer be left up to the people who come in and out of your life. Be loved by Him, so that your spouse's deficiencies no longer cause you to be deficient. You can be loved by Him so that you don't expect what people cannot give. You are not defined by the one you love as much as you are by the One who loves you.

16

THE DANGER OF KEEPING SECRETS

The Woman at the Well came to the well in the middle of the day. This is significant. Women in her day always came to the well early in the day, but she came during the hottest part of the day. Was she desperate for water? Was she unaware of the time? I think she came because she knew nobody would be there. I think she wanted to be alone. And I think she wanted to be alone for a reason. She knew the life she was living. She knew the man she was sleeping with was not her husband, and it was having an effect on her. Maybe the people in the town of Sychar thought she was married, but she knew the truth. We can assume they didn't know the truth of her situation because if they had known she was sleeping with a man who did not belong to her by marriage, they could have punished her according to the law. But the fact that she is not punished means they don't know for sure. But she does. And it isolates her. It affects her confidence. It makes her come to the well alone.

Sexual secrets can cause us to isolate ourselves. This woman was not under the social pressure of her culture at the time she comes to the well. Remember, nobody knows her secret life. But she knows, and something about keeping that secret is weighing her down. She never talks about it. In her day, she couldn't talk about it unless she wanted to invite severe punishment. She was imprisoned.

Incarcerated by her secrecy. All of us are free to do what we want. We actually have the freedom to sleep with whom we want to and do what we want to do. That's the power of choice that we appeal to whenever this subject of sex and sexual immorality comes up. We say we are free, but the reality is that our freedom to do what we want does not allow us to be free of the consequences of our decisions. This woman was imprisoned by her freedom. She was not free to claim her lover as her own husband. She was not free to interact with him publicly. Her decision to live a secret intimate life with him affected her public life. What about you? Are you imprisoned by your own freedom? You are free to look at whatever websites you want. You are free to talk to whoever you want. You are free to go out with whoever you want. And you are certainly free to sleep with whoever you want. As long as no one knows, there will be no consequences, right? Well, think again. How many times have you felt alone in your struggle to resist that woman at work who keeps flirting with you? How many times have you felt terrible about not telling that guy to stop telling you how beautiful you are? How many times have you felt all alone as you struggle to keep that affair from everyone? It's not just the cheating that's hurting you. It's not just the hiding that's hurting you. It's the secret. This woman came to the Well with a secret. Our sexual secrets are spirit breaking. They hurt us because they isolate us from community. They hurt us because we end up looking for what we need all by ourselves, and none of us live our best lives by ourselves.

The Well was a community place especially for the women to gather. They would talk, laugh, and share in each other's lives. This woman could not share, because her life was not only unacceptable to them, it was really unacceptable to her. Once we come to understand the true nature and purposes of our sexuality, then the secrets must be revealed. Sin grows in the darkness. Like festering mold, it spreads in the places where light cannot challenge it. Her secret was as damaging as her relationship. So what did Jesus do? When she expressed her desire to have this "new water" for her soul, he asked her to go get her husband. In other words, he wanted her to drag her secret into the light. She could never come out of it unless she was willing to talk about it. He knew what her situation was, but he needed her to say it. It was her secret, and it was hers to reveal. She said, "I don't have a husband" which was partly true. She was not married, but Jesus was trying to get her to reveal the fact that she was sexually involved with this man. She wouldn't say it because the truth of what we are actually doing is sometimes hard to face, isn't it? When a married mother of two is cheating on her husband, it is hard to actually say the truth that she is in the process of changing the lives of her young children forever as she puts her family in jeopardy. It's hard for the married man to actually say that he is in the process of breaking his wife's heart and setting an example of infidelity for his son who looks up to him for his social cues. When you think about what you are really doing, it's hard to actually say it. This is what Jesus was trying to get her to say. He wanted her to just say it. Not because it would change anything but because it would be the start of a change. You cannot conquer what you cannot con-fess. Jesus being the compassionate Savior, did not force her confession. In fact, when she gave this half-answer, he met her halfway. He said, "You have said it well. You have no husband. You have had five husbands and the man you are with now is not yours." Jesus helps her say it. He helps her to drag her heavy secrets into the light so she can begin to live again. This is the power of confession.

Confession is a scary thing. It means that I have to give voice to what may be unspeakable. Confession means that I have to name what action I have taken, even if it means hurting the people that I love or facing the reality that I may be hurting myself. Confession is not easy, which is why this Woman at the Well did not fully confess. Or did she? Though she never said she was sleeping with a man that was not her husband, her answer implied it. She gave a half answer because the full truth was too much to bear. And yet, Jesus offers her grace. Why does she get grace when she doesn't seem to meet the requirements? In the Bible, it says, "If we confess our sins, he is faithful and just to forgive us of all our sins and cleanse us from all unrighteousness." This woman never fully confessed so why does she receive full forgiveness? Here's why. Confession is much more than simply saying something. Confession is not just saying you did something. It really has more to do with how you view what you did. Confession, in the biblical sense, literally means "to agree or to say the same thing." The confession that Christ requires from us is not a mere statement about our wrong. Anyone can do that, especially if there are terrible consequences to pay for your wrong. But true confession is when we agree with God about our actions. We have to see our actions through His perspective and then agree with His perspective. That's true confession. We have to agree that our actions hurt our spouse. We have to agree that the affair has ruptured the relationship. We have to agree that our sexual behavior does have serious effects on us and the people connected to us. God is not looking for an apology. He is looking for agreement.

This is why when we simply say we are sorry for messing up we can feel just as messed up as we did before we confessed. It is because deep down inside we have not taken the time to see if we really agree with God on the matter. God wants you to agree with Him because when you agree, you come to understand the true nature of your mistake. It is then, and only then, that you can really accept His grace. If you don't understand what you have done, why would you need grace to cover it. Forgiveness and grace is always accepted if confession precedes them. This woman confessed. Somewhere in the conversation she agreed with Jesus. Maybe the fact that she came to the Well alone was her confession. We don't know. The story does not tell us about her spilling the sordid details of her situation to Jesus. All we know is that she didn't run from Christ's confrontation.

She stayed.
She talked.
She agreed.

You and I can take a page out of this woman's book. We don't have to run. We don't have to hide our secret. We just have to agree with God that we messed up. He will agree with us, and then He will take our heavy load and set us free to accept His love and grace. Will you agree?

Jesus shows us how we can become free from the secrecy of our sexual choices. It takes courage, but it's worth the risk. Confession for us is expressed in two ways:

1. Just Say It
Talk about what you are getting ready to do before you do it. There is something powerful about declaring to yourself what you are about to do. If sexual temptation thrives on secrecy, then expose it. Try this next time you are being faced with sexual temptation. Talk it out! Say to yourself,

"I'm going to have sex with a guy who I think likes me, but I'm not sure. So I will just give him my most precious gift with hopes that he really cares about me."

Just say it!

"I'm going to put my health and future at risk by having risky, unprotected sex with some girl at my job."
Just say it!

"I'm gonna have sex with the person I barely know because I want him to like me."

Just say it!

When you say it, you reveal the truth of your decision. This confession gives you an opportunity to hear and perhaps reevaluate your choice. Confession is agreement and if you speak it, you give yourself another chance to decide if this is really what you want to do. Do you really want to hurt your children? Do you really want to give yourself to him or her?

2. Agree with Jesus
What do you do if you have already made the mistake? The dye is already cast and milk has already been spilt. The hearts have already been broken and the deed already done. What do you do now? When Jesus invited the woman to confess, it was not for his benefit. It was for hers. She needed to face the truth of what she was doing so that she could prepare for an even greater truth, His grace. Confession is not agreement with God that we are wrong. Confession is agreement with God that we can be made right. If confession is agreement that God's perspective, then what does God see when he sees our mistakes? What does God know about our messy decisions? He knows our choices will not work out the way we planned. He knows that we will live to regret that affair or hook up. He knows our hearts will break, and our lives will be negatively affected. But Jesus also knows something more. He knows that he can make things right again. When Jesus asks us to agree with Him, he is asking us to agree that He is the remedy for our sickness.

He wants us to agree that He will restore what our sexual decisions have devastated or destroyed. The power of confession is that you become free from what you have done when you realize that Jesus doesn't see you based on your actions. He sees you based on His action on your behalf. Every time Jesus sees a sinner, he sees a candidate for grace. Do you agree with what Jesus sees in you?

17

BREAKING BAD...HABITS

One of the ways that we can change our habits of sexual sin is to let the spirit of Christ interrupt us on our way to performing our habit. The Woman at the Well was on her way to do what she always had done. Christ met her and interrupted her habit. He was able to get her to focus on something greater than what she thought she needed. A practical way of beating the sexual temptation is to let the Spirit of Christ interrupt you on your way. This can be done through prayer. Prayer is the best way to interrupt your habit with the presence of Christ. When you start talking to God, you allow Him to access your spirit so that your thirst can be quenched from the inside out. Prayer is not using a bunch of fancy words, and it is not necessary for you to know a whole lot of scripture either. Prayer is simply talking to God and being aware of his presence in your life. When you pray, the Spirit of God helps you to refocus your energy and reorganize your priorities. You will find that you have more strength to resist if you let Christ interrupt you.

Another way to interrupt the habit is to talk to yourself. Sometimes we do things out of habit without actually verbalizing what we are about to do. When Jesus spoke to the woman, he was getting her to talk about the lifestyle she was living. I believe that half the stupid stuff we say, do, and think sexually, would be avoided if we just said it out loud for us to hear what we are about to do. How many men would turn the car around if they had just said out loud to themselves, "I am about to go over to this co-worker's house and cheat on my wife with her. I am about to hurt my children and damage my relationship with them"? How many women would stop themselves from making terrible sexual mistakes if they said out loud, "I am about to go over here with this guy I hardly know and have sex with him even though I don't really think I can trust him"? I don't know about you but I think we would avoid half of our crazy mistakes if we just took the time to talk it out. There is power in what you say. The Bible has a verse that says, "Death and life are the power of the tongue…" The power of the tongue is the fact that we often believe what we speak. This is one of the reasons why speeches were given before going into war. This is why coaches and team captains gather the teams into a huddle and give them a motivational speech about winning. If you have ever seen a huddle or been in a huddle, you will notice that the captain or coach will have you repeat their motivational words. Why? The power is not simply in the actual words. The power is in speaking words of victory and success. It helps to convince the team that they can actually accomplish what they are saying. Tell yourself that you will resist the temptation. Tell yourself that you can overcome. I am not proposing some magical or mystical power is inherent in your speech. Once you have allowed the presence of God to interrupt your life, and you have talked to Him, you have the power to talk yourself out of trouble and into success. We have the power to not only make our own choices but we have the power to redirect our choices when we talk to God about our struggle and when we talk to ourselves about what we are planning to do. You can do this. You will do this. Let's do this.

The Habit of Jesus
Jesus was often alone with women, yet nothing ever

happened. Well nothing sexual or romantic ever happened. I have always wondered about this. Was Jesus really a man's man? If he was, how is it that he was able to resist temptation like he did? If he was all man and all God at the same time, maybe he dipped into his divinity every time a beautiful woman came around so that he didn't give into temptation. You have to imagine some of these women had to be beautiful. I occasionally tease my wife about how beautiful the women are in that region of the world, and I know they had to be even more beautiful in Jesus time. Long wavy hair, sun-kissed skin, bodies fit by natural fitness training (they walked almost everywhere), and they could cook too! You also cannot forget that Jesus was a rock star for most of his ministry. He was followed around by the paparazzi of his day. His sermons and speeches drew more crowds than Barack Obama in the 2008 presidential campaign. He was powerful and yet he had the rebel's edge about him. You have to know Jesus had admirers. There are certain women who are attracted to powerful, influential, confident men. Do you really believe that Jesus didn't have female groupies following him around from town to town? I don't have to see it in the Bible to know that He did. He was what many women wanted. He wasn't afraid of Rome, and he wasn't afraid of the Jewish Temple leaders. It was a huge turn on! And he had many opportunities because he often was with women. There is a woman caught in adultery in John 8, and after Christ gets rid of her accusers, he is left alone with this half-dressed woman who obviously knew her way around the bedroom. There is a woman named Mary Magdalene, who had been possessed by several demons, and she traveled with him. Then there's the account of a former prostitute who had come as an uninvited guest to dinner party and started washing Jesus feet with the perfume she had bought with money from turning tricks. And then there's this woman who is alone at a well with Jesus. He had plenty opportunities. He could have extorted the woman caught in adultery. He could have abused his influence with Mary Magdalene, and he could have become the seventh lover of this Woman at the Well. Who would have known? Yet we never read, hear or even get an idea that Christ gave into temptation. How did he do that? Did he have an advantage? Did he have access to power we don't have? The answer is no.

Jesus had a habit. He had a habit that kept him out of women's beds and in people's hearts. He had a habit that kept him pure and credible. It kept him close without getting too close. Jesus saw people for who they really were. We have a struggle with temptation because we tend to idolize, fantasize, and then sexualize people. When we see a woman that is attractive, we never think about who she really is, her personality, her pain, her story, her life journey. We take what we see, and we make an idol out of it. Women do the same thing, but it may not always be as instantaneous as men, and it may also happen for different reasons. Women will often take the personality, confidence, and persona of a man and idolize, fantasize, and finally sexualize. Though we may take different paths to get there, both women and men end up in the same place of sexual temptation. **We see people for what we want. But Jesus sees people for who they really are.**

When you read about the interactions Jesus had with women, he was always clear about who they really were. He had a habit of dealing with their humanity rather than their simple sexuality. Jesus was not asexual or not attracted to women. His mission of human redemption was greater than the need to marry and have children. His ability to get around sexual temptation was largely due to his awareness of who they really were. The woman caught in adultery was not just a sexy woman who had a reputation. Not to Jesus. She was a woman who had been exploited for far too long. He saw her for who she was. The woman named Mary, who had been possessed by several demons and had no doubt done terrible and degrading thing, was not one to be taken advantage of. Not to Jesus. He saw the chaos in her soul. He saw that she was doing terrible things because she had an invasion of evil in her spirit. He saw her for who she was. The prostitute who placed with perfume on his feet was not trying to seduce him. Not to Jesus. He sees her soul, and he knows she just wants to honor him as her Savior. He saw her for who she really was. Jesus' habit of seeing people as they really were kept him from making a sexual mistake because he always kept his view on the truth of who people were. In other words, he didn't focus on the physical exclusively; he elevated his perception to the spiritual. For we never really know who a person is until we get a glimpse of their spirit which is why sleeping with a person before marriage is a mistake. Even if you are in a relationship, you have not begun the lifelong journey that marriage provides for you to see that person's spirit. We need to practice the habit of Jesus. See people for who they are and not for what you want.

When you see people as Jesus did, you will realize the person is not what you fantasize them to be. You will see that they cannot really give you what you are wanting from them. Jesus knew people and knew that what they needed was far greater than what his own flesh might have desired. His understanding of their salvation trumped any personal temptation for sexual expression. When you see people as they are, you know who to love and what extent you can love them. How do you see people? Do you see women as exclusively physically desirable? Do you see men as simply pleasurable? Do you see men as sexual conquests? Do you see women as your next sexual escapade? The way you see them will determine how you relate to them. Jesus could be with women without having to be "with" them. Can you do that? You can. You just have to stay in the presence of God enough to get His perspective. The truth is, your perspective will change everything. The next time you are tempted to look at porn, you need to think of those young ladies and men as what they truly are - exploited people in a slavery system. The next time that woman flirts with you, you will see the emptiness of her life that she would go after a married man like you. The next time you face that temptation, you will have the ability to look past what you want, to see what the other person needs. And you will realize that a sexual episode will not fulfill their need or yours. Jesus knew what was in people and what wasn't. That's why he gave all people unconditional love. Their greatest need was to know they were loved.

18

QUENCHING
YOUR THIRST

(CENTER TO CIRCUMFERENCE)

We have talked a lot about the need for a whole and satisfied spirit. We have said time and time again that sex is primarily a spiritual experience. Sexual success is tied to our spiritual success. So how does this actually happen? There is a biblical principle that will change your life if you can just believe it and practice it. In Philippians 2:13, it says, "For it is Christ that works in you both to will and to do of His good pleasure." The biblical writer tells us that our spiritual success comes from God working in us. It's not God working on us. It's a matter of God working in us. The goal is to have God to work in the deepest parts of your soul. In fact, the text says that's where the real change happens anyway. It says he works in us both to will and to do. There is a sequence here. : God works in my spirit to help me be willing. Wow! This means I don't even have to be willing to change. That's good news. The truth is, many people reading this "kinda" want to change. You are not fully there. Part of you wants to change the way you are living. The other part of you is not fully ready to leave the life you have been living because you are so used to it and maybe even dependent on it. Here is great news for you. There is someone who wants it more than you. And he is willing to help you want your change as bad as He does. He knows how hard it is for you, and he will not let you do this by yourself. In fact, he will help you want it. It is God's spirit that gives your spirit the strength to change. It's God's will that gives you the will to change. God will work in your spirit to transform your desire so that you begin to want for yourself what he wants for you. The work is done by Jesus and not by you! Your only job is to give him the little bit of willingness you have left. God will take that and give you what you need if you had the sense to know what you need. He will answer prayers your soul uttered that your lips never spoke. He will change you from the deepest part of your soul. He can change your spirit.

When your spirit is changed, then you are equipped to live differently. This is one of the keys to living successfully. You don't just think differently and then act differently. That is only part of the solution. You have to first be changed in the spirit, and then your mind is changed and you begin to think differently. Then the body carries out your new actions.

New spirit, new mind, and new activity
New will, new thoughts, new actions

That's the secret. In that precise order. All of the frustrations of taking oaths you will never keep are gone. All the shame of failed attempts at changing is over. Your only goal is to let God into your spirit so he can change you from the inside out. Remember, the hard work is God's. All you have to do is open yourself to him. Let Him in. You may say, "but I don't know how to please God." That is true. You don't know how to please God. Neither do I. I know what He wants us to be and none of us measure up. The thing is we cannot please God by ourselves. So God says to us that he can fix that. He wants to come inside of us through the presence of his Holy Spirit and please himself in us. He wants to live in us and live for

Himself in us. Our success only depends on our availability to His Spirit, and then everything we think and do will be pleasing to God. Victory is won by moving from center to circumference.

THIRST

19

BEING SATISFIED

Why stay with one person? Why have one sexual partner for the rest of your life? Why would anyone do that to himself or herself when there are so many options out there? It is a valid and honest question. Some would even argue that monogamy is not natural and while it gives me some pause, I can see their point. It just seems like in a world of such access and availability, one should be encouraged to enjoy it all. Why not? Marriage is often seen as the "old ball and chain." It is the end of freedom and sexual exploration (in some cases the end of sexual exploitation). Both men and women are taking longer to get married largely because of how marriage is viewed in today's society. The death of fun and adventure. When it comes to sexual expression, people rarely name marriage as the laboratory for adventure and thrilling experience. So why get married and why reserve sex for marriage?

I get it. Even though I am happily married and fulfilled in my relationship, I understand the arguments. It can feel like we are being restrained. When you restrain someone, you hold them back. That's what it feels like to people. It feels restraining. Nobody wants to be restrained. Our very human spirit rebels against restraint. We want to do what we want to do. Nobody likes to have restraints put on him or her. Restraints take away the power of choice. I think this is why many people don't feel compelled to pay attention to the sexual guidance of the Bible. It is human to fight for choice. It's also godly. God wants us to have choices. Slaves are restrained. Prisoners are restrained. Nobody wants to be a slave or prisoner. So if we see marriage or abstinence as restriction, we will naturally rebel. We will delay, deny, or despise it. But what if I told you God never meant for us to be restrained. The Bible states in 2 Cor. 5:14, "For the Love of Christ constrains us." This is a radical difference from restraint. When you are restrained, it's something that is placed on you. That is why you resist. But the word constrain comes from the Latin word "constringere" which means to "bind tightly together." When we abstain from sexual immorality it is not because restraints are imposed on us. We constrain ourselves. This is different than being limited by rules and standards. This work implies self-control motivated by love. The implication is that the person plays an active role rather than a passive role. In other words, we are so bound tightly together with God because of His love that we put these sexual boundaries and limitations on ourselves. It is not a restriction. It is an honor.

Restraints are put on someone to stop them from doing something. The person is passive in the process. For many people, that's what the call for abstinence feels like. The commandments of the Bible seem like restraints. And to a certain extent, they are. If a person does not know and accept the love of God, then all the instructions and commands of God are simply restrictive and antiquated. The love that God has for me motivates me to place limits on myself due to my value. This is what gives me the power to live my sexual life differently. The love motive makes me want to value myself by placing "value-based limits" on my sexuality. My acceptance of God's love allows all my essential love needs to be met so that I limit my expressions of Eros love until they can be fully expressed in marriage, which is the ultimate human arena for Agape love. Love *empowers* me to place limits.

Limits are often seen as negative things. But not all limits are bad. The rail guards on interstate highways limit us from crossing over into oncoming traffic. The safety seals on prescription drugs limit our children from accessing dangerous pills. Limits can actually produce freedom. We are free to arrive safely to our destinations because of the limitations on speed and road access. We are free to enjoy our children's laughter because of the limits we place on them to not play in the street while cars drive by. Limits are not only necessary, but they often create freedom. Love creates limits.

I have often thought about skydiving. The thought of jumping out of a plane is curiously appealing to me. I don't quite know if I am serious about it or if it's just a fantasy of mine that grows stronger as I get older. My wife has flat out told me that it's not going to happen. Not because she doesn't think I will do it. She has forbidden me to go. Why? Her answer is always; "You are not going to risk leaving me here with these two children to raise all by myself". So I have shelved my childlike desire to jump out of the plane because the love of my wife influenced me to place a limit on the risks I take. Here is a more serious example. My wife and children mean a lot to me. I love them with all my heart. My doctor told me a few years ago that I need to watch my cholesterol. It was a bit high. So he recommended some dietary adjustments. I have not always adhered to those restrictions. That has made it a struggle to lower my cholesterol. I know I should do it. I want to live long and be healthy. I love myself. I don't think I am harboring any subconscious self-loathing. I just like hamburgers and fries. I enjoy pizza and just about anything with cheese on it. Unfortunately, they are all things that raise my cholesterol. I am presently trying to make the changes that I need to, even though my love for these things has not waned. Why am I regulating my intake of these high cholesterol foods? Because my kids have been armed with the information on how these foods contribute to my high cholesterol levels. (I wonder who did that?) They want me to live a long and healthy life. Their love makes me put limits on myself so that I can live a long and meaningful life with them. That is what I mean by love creates limits. These are not restraints put on you by someone who seeks to control you. When you are truly loved by someone, you will place certain limits on yourself in order to honor their love for you. This is the transformative power of being loved.

The motivation for this constraint is love, but it is not our love for God. Our love for God is not strong enough. Our love is not consistent enough. It is His love that causes us to abide by our self-imposed constraints. That's just how amazing His love is when you begin to understand it. You come to understand that His love is so unconditional and so liberating that it makes you want to live a better life. His love for you changes you. His love for you motivates you. His love makes you get up and try again. His love makes you forgive yourself. Our sexuality is not restrained. Our sexuality is constrained by God's love. It's our choice, but it's His Love. The unconditional love of God is what makes the difference. Temptations don't stop. Bad thoughts don't stop. In fact, they may intensify for a while as your life is reordered around the new reality you are living. The victory comes from your full acceptance of the love of God. Since sexuality is a result of agape love, your sexuality will now be only be expressed in the context of agape love. It is not the love I have for God that transforms me. If that were the case, we would all be in major trouble. Our love for God is incomplete and imperfect. We are on one day and off the next. Our love for God is often conditional. So we have to grow into our love for Him. God's love for us is the constant. And it is His love that gives us inherent value so that we make new decisions. We are "constrained" by His love.

Monogamy is another expression of this kind of love that influences limits. The choice of monogamy is a choice to limit the expression of your Eros love to one person. The critics of monogamy say that it is too limiting. Indeed it is. One could even make the argument that monogamy is not natural. Sexual attraction and appetite makes it hard for many people to limit their sexual expression with just one person. However, we have to determine what the underlying motivation is. Monogamy becomes next to impossible and perhaps irrelevant if it is not motivated by love. Think about it. True monogamy is not just reserving sexual relationship to one person exclusively, but it also includes duration of time. Monogamy says that our sexual relationship is exclusive and enduring. Almost anyone can be monogamous for a few weeks. Many people are monogamous for as long as the dating relationship lasts. However, the monogamy that marriage espouses is designed to last for as long as our spouses live. Talk about limitations! Marriage literally requires the greatest limitations on sexual exploration with other partners. When you marry someone in the Christian tradition, you vow to have sex with only one person for the rest of your life. Maybe this is where the whole "ball and chain" reference comes from. For some people, that may seem like the ultimate limitation. However, the love of the person motivates you to vow to be true to only that person. Love creates limits. These are not imposed limits. The marital vow of monogamy is not only a declaration of your love, but it is recognition of being loved by someone. When you are truly loved, you place loving limits on yourself.

If love creates loving limits, why do so many marriages end in infidelity? We cannot assume that love was not a reality in these relationships. Cheating is not a sign that a person did not feel loved by his or her spouse. Love can be present and, a person will still cheat. The problem is that somehow agape love was not in focus. When we know and accept that God unconditionally loves us, the temptation of infidelity loses its power. The love of God in and through our spouse influences us to make different choices even if the sexual appetite is striving to get the best of us. In this context of God's agape love, our sexuality is kept in perspective. The love of God makes me limit myself in order to fully experience and reciprocate that love.

This understanding has some powerful consequences. If God's love for me causes me to be constrained, then we must understand that these constraints are only for people who know and accept God's love. If you don't want to accept God's love for you, then sexual purity is not for you. If you don't accept God's love for you, then monogamy is not for you. If you don't accept God's love for you, sexual boundaries are not for you. None of what we've talked about in this book will work for you. Why? There is no reason to attempt to practice sexual purity if God's love is not the motivation. Most of us would never be successful without His love anyway. For the very small majority of people who could stay celibate or monogamous, it would not be for the right reasons. If you tried to live this sexually successful life without understanding and accepting God's love, you will only be frustrated with your failures. This life was never intended to be lived outside of or without God's love. What sense does it make to limit yourself if you are living for yourself? Why restrict yourself to one woman or one man if your life is all about pleasing yourself? It doesn't make sense.

However, if you sense deep in your soul that there has to be much more to life, then you can receive His love. This is the power of God shown in the life of Jesus. When Jesus told the woman all that she had done without condemning her, He showed her that true love knows all your faults and loves you anyway. When you know that kind of love, it changes you. It motivates you. It constrains you. It binds you to the One who loves you so much. So my marriage is not the old ball and chain. I'm glad to be constrained to one woman. If anything, I am "chained" to the One who loved me in spite of me. His love constrains me, and that is my freedom.

Jesus' love was ultimately shown to the world when He gave his life for all people. People who believed and people who still don't believe. He died for Christians and Muslims. He died for Protestants and Catholics. He died for the compassionate and the indifferent. That kind of love is what makes life worth changing. That's why 2 Cor. 5:15 picks up where verse 14 left off. It tells us "because of Christ's death for us, we no longer live for ourselves but for Him who died and rose for them". We no longer live for ourselves. We live for the One who died for us. Not to repay him. We could never do that. We live for Him because He lives in us. God will literally live in you, and His love will cause you to live differently. That's how you become a new person. In fact, the Bible goes on to say in verse 17, "Therefore if anyone is in Christ, they are a new creation; old things have passed away; behold, all things have become new". His love in us changes us so that we are no longer the same people. This newness is not always instantaneous. It's not Christian magic. The desires don't go away. The urges never leave. They aren't supposed to leave immediately. You just become different as you grow in His love. You can never really point to the exact date when a child has a growth spurt. You don't know when they outgrew that shirt you bought them a few months ago. But you know they grew. They changed. That's how it works. Jesus once told a man named Nicodemus about how this spiritual change works. Jesus taught that the work of the Spirit resembled the wind. You can't always explain where the wind began and how far it will blow, but you see its effects. When you accept God's love for you, it will show up in your life. Not always immediately, but eventually. You're still human. You will still deal with temptation and failure. The difference is that you have a divine purpose to live for because you realize God sent his Son to die so that you can truly live. His love constrains and sustains you.

20

WHEN DO YOU KNOW YOU ARE IN LOVE?

Love requires knowledge. The way you know you are loved is when people know things about you that are not lovable, but they keep loving you. This Woman at the Well had begun to figure out that there was something special about this man who was speaking to her. He was so kind, so engaging, so non-judgmental, and so different than all the men she had previously known. She found herself leaning in to every word he said. The amazing thing was that he knew everything about her. He knew her past, and he seemed to understand her pain. He was aware of her failures and her relationship. He knew her lifestyle, and he understood her life choices. He knew what happened to her and why she had done things she had done. He knew everything. This should have scared her to death. She had come to the Well at noon to escape the prying eyes and the suspicious questions of the people of her town, but then she ran into a man who she had never met before, yet knew her better than anyone else. Instead of being frightened or intimidated by his full knowledge of her, she was strangely at peace. Because while this man knew everything about her, he did not condemn her. He knew everything about her, and yet still talked to her. What he knew about her could have caused him to take up a stone, but instead he offers her a new life. **Love knows who you really are and loves you anyway.**

This woman said, " I know that when the Messiah comes, who is called the Christ, he will tell us all things". Jesus then glances at her with a look of pure love and declares, "It's me, the Messiah." It was amazing that he knew everything about her, but the most amazing things was that he knew everything about her, and he was the Messiah. Perhaps she should have been so embarrassed and so scared that her past lay bare before the Savior of the World, but still she feels no condemnation. Perfect love had perfect knowledge of her, and she knew it. She would never be the same because she was completely known by God and yet completely loved by God.

When you know you are completely known yet completely loved, it changes you from the inside out. The thirst of your soul is quenched when you understand that God knows everything and still loves you. **Experiencing the uncompromising, unwavering, unconditional love of God radically alters the trajectory of your life.** This understanding of His love allows you to understand your value. You begin to understand that God loves the real you. All of our lives, we experience love based on who we are, what we do, how we act, or even why we live the way we live. God's love does not change. His love does not adjust to our betrayals or rejection. It doesn't shift based on our behavior. The love Jesus shows remains the same. Agape love never changes; it changes you.

Here is where the transformation of the woman's soul begins. Jesus had begun to place that "hot springs" of his presence in her spirit. You can tell because her mood shifted. Her tone changed. She began to experience what Jesus has been offering her the entire time. Her thirst was finally being quenched. Her spirit was being refreshed. From the inside, she was beginning to feel... satisfied. There are three things that she experienced that quenched her thirst that day, and Jesus wants you and I to experience these as well.

1. Experience the uncompromising, unwavering, unconditional love of God

God loves you unconditionally; therefore, it doesn't matter what mistakes or decisions you have made. You are still loved and no matter what you do, you will always be loved. No conditions. When was the last time you experienced that kind of love? Who is the last person who loved you like that? I know you may be searching your mental hard drive to think about those one or two people in your life that were always there for you. Maybe your grandmother or your childhood best friend. Maybe you think you've experienced this kind of agape love from one of your teachers or mentors. But I would like to challenge you by saying that I doubt it. They may know you, but they don't know everything. They don't know every thought that crossed your mind. They don't know about the intentions you had and the things you would have done if you could have done them. They don't know all the secrets and all the dirt. They love you but they don't know everything. This is why perfect agape love can only be expressed and experienced fully through God. He knows it all, and He still loves. This speaks not only to the kind of love it is but how long it lasts. No matter what you and I do to God, his love still attaches no conditions and never changes. He loves just because not because of what you do. God's love is not because of you but in spite of you.

This love is a spiritual reality because it is not based on physical or mental. It is essential love. You are loved from the inside out. From center to circumference. This reality starts in your Spirit. Once you know this for yourself, you begin to believe that you are spiritually valuable. You are not just physically valuable. You are not just intellectually valuable, but you are valuable because you are alive. You are essential to the world. You have value that is not tied to anything or anyone. Your value is completely confirmed and affirmed by God's love.

Here's how it works. Your value is not from what people say about you or do to you. It is to not just a mental or physical thing. Your value is a spiritual reality. Your spirit tells your mind that you are valuable. When your mind is convinced of this truth, then your body will simply live out that truth in the sexual decisions you make. Your value is firmly established in your spirit. This allows you to make up your mind and change your thoughts about who you are and what you deserve. The power of changing your thoughts is not in your mind. It is in your spirit. So if your spirit is essentially valuable because of the agape love of God, then your thinking will change. When your thinking changes, your physical and sexual choices will change. The problem that we have with sexuality in today's culture is that we have reversed the order of finding value. Value can never flow from body to spirit. Your value is not based on your curves or net worth. You are valuable because of the God who loves you and gave his life for you. When you accept your value in your spirit, then the transformation begins. When this acceptance of value is in your spirit, you can begin to return your sexuality to the original context of agape love that it is supposed to thrive in.

2. You Accept and Apply Grace

We don't like grace. We would rather choose sin. Grace is when God treats us in a way we don't deserve. Our problem is that we choose one of two responses to his offer. We say, "I don't deserve his kindness or forgiveness so I can't accept his offer of grace." While this is true, it leaves us in the mess of our own mistakes and decisions. Acknowledging our guilt doesn't fix our problem. When we look at ourselves in such a dire way, we remain thirsty and in need of redemption. The other response to God's grace is, "I deserve to do what I want so I don't need His grace." This response leads us to living life without any boundaries and ultimately without any satisfaction. There is another response to His grace. We can simply say, "I don't deserve it, but I need it." Like the Woman at the Well, we need what God offers us through Jesus. While God gives us grace he does not apply grace for us. When a doctor gives you medicine with an explanation of how it will help to heal your illness, he expects you to fill the prescription and take the medicine. He cannot make you take the pills. He cannot fill the prescription for you. The medicine only helps, if you take it. When we talk about grace, we often see it as some ethereal thing that God does for us. We treat it like Christian magic. But grace is useless if we don't actively apply it.

We accept grace mentally, but we don't actually apply it to our situations. Many people believe that God forgives, but they don't actually forgive themselves. We are often way harder on ourselves than God is. Applying grace is believing that you have another chance. Applying grace is not being so hard on yourself. In order to apply grace, we have to practice self-compassion and self-forgiveness. The way you think about yourself in relationship to your failure may determine if you will repeat the same failure. Neuroscientists are saying that our thoughts about our failures are just as damaging as our actual failures. Grace applied tells me that it's okay to not be okay. But it's not okay to stop trying to be okay. Grace applied helps me to stop negative thinking about myself so that I can be free to a new version of myself. If you can think with grace orientation, you can have hopeful thoughts about the future.

3. Experience the Presence of Jesus in Your Spirit
The same Jesus that spoke to that lady that day desires to live in us. He wants to love us from the inside out, and he accomplished this through the presence of his spirit. Now there are two things about his spirit that should encourage you. First, the Holy Spirit, who is the presence of God on earth wants to live inside you. This means that all the love God has for you he doesn't just simply lavish on you from

Heaven, but he actually brings that love inside your spirit. This means that God's infinite and unconditional love can be accessed from your very spirit. Wow! God in me! Unconditional Love inside me! When this happens, you no longer need that kind of love from the outside because it resides in you. When you become thirsty for acceptance and approval, you can access that from God's spirit in you. When your self-esteem and self-worth have taken a hit, you can dip down in the fountains of your own spirit to find that life-giving presence of God in you. You don't have to rely on empty promises and relationships that never quite turn out to be as you wished. This reality of God in you is how you move from temporary happiness to perpetual joy. Peace of mind replaces anxiety and uncertainty. Your source of identity, strength, and love flows from the center of your soul and shows up in your daily decisions. When God's spirit fills your spirit, you will date the right people. You will not put unfair expectations on people who were never meant to make you happy. You will be free from the tyranny of your own emptiness. Life really begins when you receive this precious gift of God in you.

You can live this new type of life if you are tired of running out of what your soul needs. If you are tired of relationships draining you instead of giving you life. If you realize that your sex life is not making you feel as loved as you thought it would. If you are honest enough to admit that you have been using sex and your relationships to make you feel whole, you don't have to live like that anymore. Jesus promises that if you let him, he will satisfy all your needs by coming into your life. He will be your thirst quencher. He will meet all your deepest needs for love and acceptance. Jesus knows you, what you have done, and what you need. He is still offering to quench your thirst.

THIRST

21

LEAVE YOUR BUCKET BEHIND

Everything changes when you really meet Jesus. The Woman knew that Jesus knew everything about her. Feeling fully loved and fully known, her spiritual fountain was bubbling over with joy and excitement. She had come to the well for much needed water. She had physical needs that had to be met. She needed the water to wash. She had to drink and bathe. There were plants to water and food to cook. But all her previously important needs had been sidelined. She had found love, real love. Her appetite had left her. Her focus on the water had given way to her overwhelming spiritual satisfaction. What she did next was remarkable. She left Jesus standing there and ran back to the town shouting, "Come see a man who told me everything I ever did". She was so full of joy and freedom that she ran to tell everyone about Jesus. But even more remarkable than that was what she left behind with Jesus.

She left her bucket

She left behind what she thought she needed to meet her own needs

She left behind the very thing that she used to quench her thirst

Once she met Jesus and was filled with His love, His grace, and His spirit, she didn't need what she had previously needed to be full. She left it behind because the bucket could no longer contain what she really needed. Why do you need a bucket for water when you have natural springs of water inside of you? Her natural thirst had given way to her spiritual thirst. The physical need had been superseded by her spiritual satisfaction. She left her bucket behind. When you let Jesus lavish you with His love, give you His grace, and fill you with His spirit, you will leave your bucket behind too. It's just what naturally happens when your spirit is satisfied. When your thirst has been quenched, you leave some things you previously thought you needed, behind.

You can leave the sexual partner, behind.
You can leave that affair, behind.
You can leave that porn, behind.
You can leave that lustful pattern, behind.
You can leave the promiscuity, behind.

What Jesus did for the woman was also a pattern for how we can live our new lives as well. It is important to note that Jesus never asked the Woman to change her lifestyle. He never told her to go home and break up with her lover. He never instructed her to change her behavior. This is intentional. If Jesus had instructed her to change her behavior before she had received his precious gift, he would have been setting her up for defeat because none of us can experience sustainable behavior change without first being changed internally. If she had gone home and broken off the scandalous affair, without being filled in her spirit, she would have run out of resources to sustain her new lifestyle and eventually, returned to her past habits. Jesus shows us how this new thirst-quenching life works. Jesus did not instruct her to change her behavior because he knew that if her spirit's thirst was quenched, her behavior would change eventually, and she would never go back to her past. Jesus knew that new life must precede new decisions and not the other way around. He knew that the resources she would need to lead a new life would have to come from the right source. So Jesus does not give her exact steps on what to do. He quenches the thirst and then trusts the Spirit of God inside her to do the rest. That's how God works with us. Whenever we prioritize changing our behavior, we forget that the only way to make sustainable changes, is to first be changed. If life flows from the center to circumference, then change does too. Jesus did not really come to change her lifestyle; he came to change her life and as a result, her lifestyle would change. This is what Jesus wants to do for you and me. His primary goal is not to alter our behavior, and the natural consequence will be that we will leave all of our buckets behind.

The love the woman at the Well had experienced in the presence of Jesus caused her natural desire to be put in its rightful place. When you're full of his love, hope, and grace, then your natural desires for sexual expression will be regulated by his love. God does not take away your sexual desires. Why would God do that when he is the one who gave you sexual desire? I am not suggesting that when your spirit is full with God that you will no longer be tempted or desirous of sexual expression. God does not replace or remove sexual desire. In fact, if you are married, God's spirit in you will fuel your passion for sexual expression with your spouse that is beyond your natural desire. The spirit of God in your spirit fills you in a way that your thirst for sexual pleasure is put into proper perspective. The woman left her bucket because she was already full. She would need water again. Her natural need to drink, bathe, wash, and clean would not go away. But now all of those needs took a backseat to her new found love. They were not as important to her new life she had found. So she left the bucket behind to tell everyone and show everyone that she was full. God destined you and I to be so full of Him that we had no need to depend fully on any other flawed human being for unconditional love.

Have you been carrying a bucket that has been weighing you down? Have you been carrying a secret around? Have you been carrying a lifestyle that has been weighing you down? Have you been carrying around the weight of sexual experiences that make you feel better about yourself for a while but leave you empty and dissatisfied? Do you hide in the shadows in order to enjoy moments of stolen passion? Are you tired of having to come back to the same wells and never being satisfied? If you are tired of the weight and the emptiness, you no longer have to live that way. Stop going to the same well expecting a different experience. Sexual relationships were never designed to quench your spirit's thirst. Romance was never created to fulfill your soul's desire. They are limited and finite. The only experience that will satisfy your thirst is when God fills the space in you that was designed for him and him alone. If you give Jesus permission, he will fill you from the inside out. When this happens, the change will show up in the way you live your life.

I don't think the woman planned to leave her bucket and run to the town. I think she was simply being driven by the fullness of her spirit. Remember that natural springs begin their activity beneath the surface and once the temperature and pressure get to a certain level, what was once beneath the surface bubbles and explodes to the surface. While Jesus was talking with her, hope was bubbling under the surface. While Jesus was spending time with her, grace was working under the surface. While Jesus was listening to her, love was bubbling under the surface. Once she found out that He knew everything about her and still showed her mercy, what had been building under the surface could no longer be held or suppressed. Her spiritual fountain exploded into a testimony of how the Savior of the world met her and changed her life. Her internal change resulted in an external display. She ran to tell everyone that something new and exciting had happened inside her, and she invited them to come and have the same experience.

I know why this woman was so excited. I know why she couldn't keep it to herself. I was excited the day I realized that Jesus knew all about my life and still loved me. I remember the first time. Joy bubbled to my surface, and I just couldn't help but make changes in my life. It was not a religious experience. I had been raised in the Church and was religious all my life. It was not even an emotional experience. I didn't hear a sermon or song that moved me deeply. I just remember reading a verse of the Bible while rushing to one of my college classes. I quickly rattled off a half-baked prayer and was getting ready to rush out the door, but I felt impressed to sit down again and just think about what I had read. I wish I could tell you that I remember the scripture I had read, but I don't. I wasn't really paying attention. I was just doing my religious duty. Read a scripture, say a prayer, and live your life. But something happened that day. I just sat in silence, and I heard God say to me over and over again, "Do you know that I love you? No matter what you do, I love you." Over and over again, I felt this phrase coming from God. I didn't hear a voice. There was no sound. Just an undeniable truth was placed deep down inside of me. Finally in that wonderful silence I realized I was loved by God not because of what I had done for him but because of what He had done for me. The message I had heard with my ears and studied in the bible with my mind had finally made sense. I had to receive and believe in the essence of my being. I heard it physically and pondered it mentally, but now it was a spiritual reality. I could feel a release of the pressure of self-condemnation beginning to dissipate. I felt lighter and happier. I felt free to live without the fear and shame that had perpetuated so many bad decisions. What happened that day set the stage for a brand new life. New life had bubbled up to the surface when Christ's presence penetrated through to my spirit. It was at that moment that scripture came to my mind that I had read but never really paid attention to before. The text was Romans 8:38, 39 which is now my favorite text of scripture and it says "For I am sure that neither death nor life, nor angels nor principalities, nor powers, nor things present nor things to come, nor height nor depth, nor any other created thing, shall be able to separate us from the love of God which is in Christ Jesus our Lord." I didn't just understand that I was loved. I knew I was loved, from the inside out.

God does not quench your thirst by giving you something in your spirit. He does not give you some special knowledge to help you live life better. He does not give you some special power to resist sexual temptation or make better relationship decisions. God gives you this eternal resource of life by giving you Himself. In other words, God gives us Himself and as a result, all our spirit's needs are fully satisfied. When we dare to hope again and accept the grace and unconditional love of Christ, we accept the invitation of Christ to live inside of us by the presence of His spirit. Christ is our fountain and our resource for life. He doesn't give us power; he is our power.

When you read the story of this woman with Jesus you will discover that Jesus never tells her that she had received the spring of water he had promised her. He never tells her what to do to receive it, and he never indicates when she would receive it. Jesus does not make a pronouncement to declare to her that he had granted her request for this special water. In fact, after he brings up her sexual lifestyle, he never mentions his offer again. What the Woman didn't know was that Jesus had been placing that fountain of living water inside her spirit the whole time. She received her precious gift by just staying there talking with Jesus. What she didn't realize is that her change was happening by just being with Him and by the time Jesus was done, the Spirit of God was working inside her. He didn't have to proclaim it. He just did it. How do we know it happened? She left her bucket and told everyone about Jesus. If you just stay with Jesus, you will find him moving from talking to you, to living inside you. The change begins by just staying with him.

In the end of this Woman's story, we don't see all of her issues resolved. The writer does not tell us that she went home and broke it off with her lover. There is no mention of Jesus telling her to change her ways. The story only ends with her sharing her experience with Jesus, and her testimony results in many people believing in Jesus. No perfect ending. Why don't we hear about what happened to this Woman after she met Jesus? I think we don't hear the rest of her story because of two reasons. First, it could be that she went straight home and changed her lifestyle immediately or maybe it happened gradually over the next few weeks and months. That's the way life works. Sometimes we change immediately, and in many ways it happens gradually. It would have been nice to know that she altered her decisions right away, but we don't know that for sure. Either way, we know she wanted an internal change, and Jesus granted her desire. The fact that she met Jesus and she ended up leaving her bucket tells us that something happened because Jesus never offers something to willing people and not give it to them. We know she met Jesus, and we know she knew Jesus. That was enough for her whole life to change.

Secondly, her story is really our story. Our story is still being written. We, like this woman, all have our buckets. We all have used sex and sexuality to meet our own spiritual needs. We now have the opportunity to co-write the last chapter of our story. We can decide if we want to remain thirsty or if we will be filled. We can decide if we will allow our natural appetites to derail our destiny. We can decide if we will keep going to our sexuality to deal with our insecurity. It's up to us. This woman's story doesn't end in resolution because our story is not yet resolved until we make our decision. Will you keep trying to quench a spiritual thirst with your sexual appetites or will you allow Christ to fill you and love you from the inside out? It's up to you. In the meantime, He will be there waiting on you. Remember the Woman did not ask to meet Jesus. She just went to the same well one day and ran into him. He will do the same for you. He will meet you at your point of need because he always gets there before you do. He's hoping you will let Him quench your thirst.

FINAL WORDS

The Woman came to the well because she ran out of what she thought she needed. She ran out of water and came to get a refill. She thought that she would simply retrieve some water that day, but she ended up running into her Savior. This was no chance meeting. It was not a coincidence or an accident. It was a divine appointment. She was supposed to meet Jesus. But the reason she meets Jesus is because she runs out of what she needs. My prayer for you is that you have this same experience and encounter with Jesus for yourself. In order for this to happen, you must run out of what you think you need as well.

I want to end this book with a prayer for you. I want to pray that you will experience the same lacking and leaking that drove this Woman to the place where she met Jesus. I am not going to pray that you be successful. I am sure you are already hoping for that. I am not going to pray for you to prosper because I'm sure you are working hard on that as well. My prayer for you is that you run out. I want to pray that all of your attempts to use sex to fill your life will be unsatisfying. When this happens, we come to understand our need for something and someone far deeper. So let me pray for you…

God, I thank you for sending Jesus to this earth to meet us all at our own wells. Thank you for not waiting for our invitation to intercept at our point of need. God, I pray for all those who read this book. My prayer is not for them to enjoy the book and neither do I pray that they simply learn something new. I pray that they run out. I pray that they run out of the satisfaction of living without you. I pray that they would run out of hap-

piness in sleeping around. I pray that the excitement that affair is bringing that married person would run out. I pray the cheap security that sexual relationship is bringing that single woman would run out. I pray the affirmation that single man gets from his sexual exploits will run out. God, show them the futility of trying to quench their own spiritual thirst. Let them run out of lovers. Let them run out of everything that they are using to meet their greatest needs. May they run out of it all so they can run into You. I know that when they run into You, they will run into their Savior. Fill them with your hope. Fill them with your grace, and fill them with your Agape love. God fill them with You so they will thirst only for You. Thank You, Fountain of Living Water, in Jesus Name. Let it be (Amen)

The End

WORKS CITED

Chapter 2:
Maia Szalavitz, *"How Orphanages Kill Babies and Why No Child Under 5 Should Be in One"*, Huffington Post, November 2011.

Sue Gerhardt, *Why Love Matters: How Affection Shapes a Baby's Brain.* New York: Brunner-Routledge, 2004, P. 110.

Chapter 3:
Amy Schumer, *The Girl with the Lower Back Tattoo*, Simon and Schuster, 2016.

Daily Mail Reporter, *"Four Times Divorced Sean Bean says he has given up on Marriage"* April 21, 2011.

Max Lucado, *God Came Near*, Nashville: Thomas Nelson Publishing, 2004.

Chapter 5:
Elahe Izadi, *"A Bad Marriage Can Literally Break Your Heart"*, Washington Post, November 20, 2014.

Chapter 6:
Kwame Vanderhorst, *Smellin' Ourselves: What Men Need to Understand About Ourselves and Our Women. Washington D.C.: Hotep Productions, 1998.*

Kelly McGonigal, *The Will Power Instinct*, New York: Penguin Publishing Group, 2012.

Brene Brown, *Daring Greatly*. New York: Penguin Publishing Group, 2012.

Chapter 14:

Lyrics from "Stay with Me" by Sam Smith

Chapter 15:
Kelly McGonigal, *The Will Power Instinct*, New York: Penguin Publishing Group, 2012.

THIRST

ABOUT THE AUTHOR

C. Wesley Knight, D.Min. is a pastor, preacher, mentor, and change agent. He has preached in various parts of the world with a passion to see lives and communities changed. Wesley currently serves as the assistant Professor of Preaching and Religion at Oakwood University in Huntsville, AL. He is married to Stephanie and they have two amazing kids.

QUENCHING YOUR DEEPEST DESIRE

CONNECT WITH WESLEY

LET'S STAY CONNECTED!
Facebook | Wesley Knight
Twitter | @cwesleyknight
Instagram | @cwesleyknight
YouTube | C. Wesley Knight
Website | www.wesleyknight.org